Scribblers & Scoundrels

BOOKS BY CHARLES HAMILTON

Cry of the Thunderbird: The American Indian's Own Story (New York, 1950)

Men of the Underworld: The Professional Criminal's Own Story (New York, 1952)

Braddock's Defeat (Norman, Oklahoma, 1959)

Collecting Autographs and Manuscripts (Norman, Oklahoma, 1961)

Lincoln in Photographs: An Album of Every Known Pose (Norman, Oklahoma, 1963, with Lloyd Ostendorf)

The Robot That Helped to Make a President (New York, 1965)

Scribblers and Scoundrels (New York, 1968)

Scribblers & Scoundrels

CHARLES HAMILTON

Introduction by

DIANE HAMILTON

PAUL S. ERIKSSON, INC. NEW YORK

INTRODUCTION

That bundle of letters in your bureau drawer may be worth a lot of money to someone, but be careful when you untie the pink ribbons. They could set off an explosion, especially if someone doesn't want them sold at auction.

Why should anyone want to suppress a lot of old letters? For the same reason that artists often destroy those creations which they feel are not up to their best efforts, that poets fill wastebaskets with verses that don't fully reflect their genius, that authors jettison entire manuscripts they think are not good enough to submit to a publisher. It is with the same emotions, if not for the same motives, that politicians and public figures try to suppress letters or documents in which they express themselves too vehemently or too honestly.

But to my husband, the author, every letter or document that comes to him represents history and, as a manuscript dealer, he must act as a sort of historian without portfolio. It is his job to preserve all written records entrusted to him and see that they go to someone who will feel the same responsibility. Unpublished letters, manuscripts, poems, documents, reports, all must be dealt with impartially, without the prejudice and sentimentality that threaten the recording of history. But his job is made difficult by some of the misguided, often very powerful, people who try to stop the sale of letters, and sometimes succeed.

It is about some of these self-appointed censors of history that the author tells in this book, and about his disputes with them. An emotional letter is the most candid relic that one can find of a famous man, though it is often the one thing that the writer would least wish to appear for sale at public auction.

So wildly sought are intimate letters and manuscripts that they have long been fair game for thieves as well as collectors. And an obviously limited supply has even produced a number of notorious forgers who found it profitable to turn out more documents to meet the great demand. Charles Hamilton is always a mark for vendors of these stolen or forged papers, and some of his most exciting experiences with rogues are recorded in these pages.

The voracity for choice documents which provide an insight into history or uncover secret motives has brought about a bull market in rare manuscripts. The author tells how to bid for them at auction and how to collect them for investment and profit, but he also has some advice for the collector of small means. [Avoid the trite, the uninteresting, and seek the colorful and spectacular—anything that provides an intimate insight into history.]

If the youthful autograph collectors of today, who so often seek only trivial signatures or accumulate dismal collections of signed first-day covers or inscribed photographs, will heed Charles Hamilton's advice, then the coming generation of collectors and historians will leave for posterity a rich heritage of the most revealing and important ideas of the greatest men of our era.

Diane Hamilton

New York, N.Y.
March 19, 1968

TABLE OF CONTENTS

vii

CONTENTS

AFFAIRS OF STATE

The confidential letters and papers of Presidents and kings and dictators are true fragments of history. Often grist for the newspapers, they may at times become head-line scandals.

A secret communication signed by the Soviet premier, a stolen letter of Abraham Lincoln, a flowing, handwritten note from Jacqueline Kennedy to Lady Bird Johnson. . . .

All such documents are more than mere scraps of paper. They can, and often do, change the course of state.

1

MY CLASH WITH THE "GESTAPO"

Half of this story may be found in the records of the
Secret Service and the FBI. The other half I will set
down here for the first time.

On the afternoon of May 17, 1965, I got a telephone
call from The White House in Washington, D.C. It was
Elizabeth Carpenter, press secretary and staff director
for Lady Bird Johnson. I asked my assistant to handle it,
if possible, but was told that Mrs. Carpenter wished to
speak to me privately.

I would do almost anything, go to almost any length,
to avoid talking on the telephone. Since I was a boy I
have had a sort of hero-worship for every President, even
when I didn't agree with his politics. But a call from The
White House for me has one thing in common with any
other telephone call—it is painful and it is to be avoided,
if possible. In my own version of history I credit the
murderous de Medicis and not Alexander Graham Bell
with the invention of this unique torture instrument.

I turned the call over to my friend and press agent,

Harvey V. Fondiller, who is an expert at rescuing me from such situations and giving me all the credit afterward.

Mrs. Carpenter explained to Harvey that the First Lady had read in the newspapers that I was offering at auction a letter of Jacqueline Kennedy to Mrs. Johnson. Harvey confirmed the report, and Mrs. Carpenter demanded to know the name of the "owner" of the letter. Because it is against my policy to reveal a consignor's identity without his consent, we refused to give Mrs. Carpenter the name. She then demanded the immediate return of the note, which she insisted was the "rightful property" of Mrs. Johnson. We had to refuse her again. But we did promise to check immediately on Mrs. Johnson's claim and find out who really did own the letter.

The object of this peremptory White House demand was a rather innocuous missive of two pages in which Mrs. Kennedy invited Mrs. Johnson to join a party of friends to watch one of the now-famous Kennedy-Nixon debates on television. Liberally punctuated with the artistic dashes which Mrs. Kennedy uses in place of periods, and penned in her beautiful and delicate script, the letter read:

"Dear Mrs. Johnson:—

"I just heard you were going to be in town today and wondered if you would like to listen to the Debate with us—

"I'm having a Listening Party at 1028 Connecticut

Ave and would love it if you came and brought anyone you like—

"But—I expect you are exhausted from your travels (I loved your story in *N.Y. Herald Tribune*) and are looking forward to relaxing & watching TV at home—If so, I understand perfectly!

"As always
                    "JACKIE"

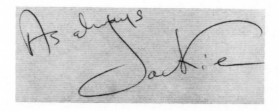

Signature on letter of Mrs. Kennedy to Mrs. Johnson.

I wondered why Mrs. Johnson was so frantic to get this little note. The phone call from her secretary had been almost threatening, certainly not a call to ignore. Then I reflected that in my auction catalogue I had placed on the letter an estimated value of $400. And I recalled that Mrs. Johnson prided herself on being a sharp business woman. I once read a letter in which she wrote enthusiastically of her greatest ambition—to take a course in bookkeeping, so that she could keep better track of the family finances. Obviously, if this letter was worth $400 she wanted it.

I tried unsuccessfully to reach the consignor of the letter, Mrs. Lucianne Cummings, so that I could check the ownership. When Mrs. Cummings had turned the letter over to me to sell, she said, "Mrs. Johnson gave it to me during the Presidential campaign, when I was working at her headquarters." I remembered her exact words, because it struck me as a very gracious thing for Mrs. Johnson to do, and I had previously been under the impression that she never gave away anything—not even a letter of a then-Senator's wife.

All that evening and the next morning we tried to get in touch with Mrs. Cummings, but she was out of town. The following afternoon at precisely 1:30 P.M. I got an airmail, special delivery letter from The White House. Letters from The White House unnerve me even more than phone calls, and I had a hunch that this particular communication was going to be unpleasant.

I was right.

Mrs. Carpenter wrote, in part: "Mrs. Johnson is absolutely certain that she has never given away any letter sent to her by Mrs. Kennedy—in fact it has always been her policy to retain all letters sent to her personally.

"Mrs. Johnson assumes that anyone who writes a personal letter to her does so with the understanding that it will remain a personal matter. To treat correspondence otherwise is, of course, an invasion of privacy."

The letter concluded with the royal command that I restore Mrs. Kennedy's note "without delay" to its "rightful owner."

Although I was irked by the tone of Mrs. Carpenter's letter, I pushed harder than ever in my effort to locate Mrs. Cummings. If, as Mrs. Carpenter insisted, the letter had not been presented to Mrs. Cummings, then it certainly belonged to the First Lady and I was morally obligated to return it at once. So far as Mrs. Carpenter's gibe about the "invasion of privacy" went, I knew, if The White House lawyers did not, that this provision in our law does not apply to high-ranking public servants.

I had a hunch that Mrs. Johnson wouldn't stop at a mere phone call and a letter, so that afternoon when I left my office I took the precaution of folding up and slipping into my pocket the small and innocuous-looking missive of Mrs. Kennedy.

Not more than ten minutes after I walked out of the shop, two Secret Service men entered, accosted our vice president, H. Keith Thompson, Jr., and demanded that he turn the Mrs. Kennedy note over to them. They explained that they were emissaries from the First Lady.

"I don't think it's in the shop," said Keith. "And, if it were, I couldn't hand it over to you without Mr. Hamilton's okay."

"Can you get his okay?" asked one.

Keith telephoned me to explain the situation. I was at first incredulous, then furious. I could see no excuse for the First Lady to resort to such strong-arm tactics.

"Ask them to come back tomorrow at 11:00 in the morning," I told Keith. "By then I will certainly have checked on the letter, and if it is the property of Lady Bird Johnson I'll turn it over to them."

For a while I smoldered, volcano-like. I have never liked the idea of a secret police force, and I saw no reason at all why they should be sicked on me by the First Lady. Furthermore, I was given only three hours after receiving Mrs. Carpenter's letter to deliver an answer to Washington, D.C. From the highest office in the nation, I felt, the President and Mrs. Johnson were using their immense authority to bully me.

I dislike bullies intensely. And I love a good fight. The smaller my chances of winning the more rewarding to me is the battle.

So that evening I telephoned Harvey Fondiller and asked him to come to my apartment. Together we drafted a strongly worded telegram stating that Mrs. Johnson had sent the Secret Service to seize a letter of Mrs. Kennedy which I was offering at auction, and that I was not, as yet, certain that I would turn it over to them. Copies of this telegram were immediately dispatched to *The New York Times*, the Associated Press, United Press International, and *Time* magazine.

At nine o'clock the next morning, after two days of constant effort, we finally located Mrs. Cummings, who explained: "Mrs. Johnson did give me the letter, as I told you, but she really gave it to me to answer for her. Since she declined Jackie's invitation, I had no idea she would want it back. If she's sent the Secret Service after it, in heaven's name, give it to her!"

Secret Service agents leaving Hamilton's shop after refusing to pick up letter of Mrs. John F. Kennedy to Mrs. Lyndon B. Johnson.

By ten o'clock my shop was already crowded with newsmen and television cameras.

Just before eleven, Keith Thompson spotted the two Secret Service men skulking about the store, looking warily and uncertainly inside at the huge battery of cameras and waiting reporters. Finally they turned away, apparently deciding to move on. But Keith was too quick for them. He dashed to the door.

"Hello, gentlemen!" he cried. "Come right in. We're expecting you!"

Keith introduced them to me.

"I have the letter here," I said, "ready to hand over to you."

Cameras were grinding.

"I am not at all sure," said one of the Secret Service men, "that we want the letter. We would like to call our office, if we may use your private phone."

As the two men made their way through the crowds of newsmen, questions were shouted at them:

"Do you run many personal errands like this for the First Lady? Are you just White House delivery boys?"

"Where do you get your authority to enter this shop and demand a letter of Mrs. Kennedy?"

"Has the President or First Lady ever used you for this kind of job before?"

To these and other questions, they shook their heads or answered, "No comment."

After about fifteen minutes in the sanctuary of my office, they emerged and explained: "We don't want the letter. We want you to send it by registered mail to Mrs. Johnson. We never intended to pick it up, anyway."

They left hurriedly, followed by a barrage of questions, all unanswered.

In interviews with the press, I described Mrs. Johnson's tactics as "Gestapo-ish."

Early in the afternoon I mailed Mrs. Kennedy's letter back to Mrs. Johnson. That should have finished the matter, but it didn't.

A postal inspector called, asking where I had mailed the note. He had instructions to keep track of it until it reached the hands of the First Lady.

The next morning a pair of FBI men walked into my shop.

"We want to know the name of the person who claimed to own the letter from Mrs. Kennedy to Mrs. Johnson," they explained.

I told them I could not disclose the consignor's identity.

"We have instructions to get the information," they said. "Suppose you think it over and let us know."

Again I was unable to contact Mrs. Cummings. I felt that I should not reveal her name without her explicit permission.

Twice the next day I was visited by the FBI. They were obviously working on a program of harassment. Each time they were more persuasive; and the more persuasive they got, the more adamant I became.

At last I reached Mrs. Cummings on the phone. "The

FBI is trying to get you," I told her. "If you would consent, without giving your name, to talk with one of the agents on the phone, I think you might resolve the matter once and for all. You have nothing to hide or be ashamed of."

She agreed. And, after she spoke with the FBI, she held a press conference in my showroom, explaining briefly the background to the letter.

Now I felt sure at last that the incident was closed for me. But I was wrong again. For weeks afterward I was alternately lauded and lambasted in the press. I was accused of being a money-grubber who would sell anything for a quick buck, and praised for being a Jack-the-Giant-Killer who attacked a power-mad President and First Lady all by himself.

Some of my correspondents angrily suggested that I get out of the autograph business; others urged me to run for congress.

Someday I am going to do one or the other.

2

THE LOOTED DIPLOMATIC POUCH

The document in front of me was handsomely and immaculately typed in Russian on paper watermarked with a hammer and sickle and boldly signed at the end of its eighteen pages by Premier Nikita S. Khrushchev. Moreover, it was plainly a letter of state, dated from the Kremlin on December 31, 1963, and addressed to the recently deposed president of Bolivia, Victor Paz Estenssoro.

"Who's offering this for sale?" I asked my secretary.

"A weird man with a German accent. He didn't want to tell me his name, but I'll try again."

I looked more closely at the letter that already was taking on an air of mystery. The heavy, rag stationery was magnificently embossed with the ominous hammer and sickle and laid in a handsome grey folder ornamented with the Communist emblem. Also it had all the pomp and ceremony about it one would expect in a communication from one potentate to another. I could not read a word of the text but I realized instantly it must be very important. And I knew, too, that it might contain diplomatic secrets of great significance to the Communists and the Bolivians.

My guess was that it very probably was stolen from the Russian or the Bolivian diplomatic files—perhaps pilfered right out of a courier's pouch. What I didn't know was how so potentially dangerous a document ever found its way into my office, offered for sale by a man whose motives were at best very suspicious.

Now, I have an unbreakable rule to investigate all possibly stolen letters and to go after crooks relentlessly. In my career as a dealer I have helped to send seven thieves to prison. I will spare no effort and no expense to put behind bars the man who preys on society.

But there are two exceptions to my rule. The first is in the case of material stolen from the Nazis—the second, the Communists. A few years ago a man dangled in front of me a whole archive of medieval German documents, important treaties with pendant wax seals dating back to the year 1100.

"From what museum in Germany did these come?" I asked him.

He gave me a startled and angry look. "Just exactly what do you mean?"

"I mean," I said, "what museum in Germany did you *steal* them from?"

He was silent for a moment, then he answered: "You are right. During the Second World War, I was with Patton's Second Army, in an advance tank division. We fought our way into a little town in Germany where we found a museum. We drove our tank right through the front of the building. Then we looted it. Most of the guys took whatever was made of gold or silver, but I took these because I always liked old documents."

"I'd be happy to buy them and handle them," I said. "My opinion is this. Hitler wanted war. He fought and lost and the Germans who supported him should pay the penalty. Part of the penalty is giving up some of their national treasures. Hundreds of thousands of American boys gave their lives in the war. If the Germans could restore these lives, then we should return their old documents."

"You're absolutely right. After all, Patton himself looted many of the museums in Germany of their rare and fine old weapons, all for his personal collection, and nobody has dared to ask for them back."

Although I was unable to purchase these choice historic documents from Patton's former soldier because we couldn't agree on a price, I found myself remembering that incident as my eyes ran over the Khrushchev letter.

Supposing it was stolen, then the chief loser by its publication and sale would be Communist Russia. And the Communist documents which come my way I neither ask nor care about the provenance of.

"Where is the person who brought in this letter of Nikita Khrushchev?" I asked my secretary.

"He said he would come back for your offer."

"Tell him I will give him $300."

Later, while I was out of the office, the vendor returned and accepted the check which my secretary offered him. And, at her insistence, he gave her his name and address.

I telephoned my Russian translator, and within a few hours she had furnished me with a complete translation of one of the most amazing letters ever written by a chief of state. Khrushchev had outlined the history of territorial conflicts, stressed the importance of peaceful coexistence, and proposed an international treaty for the abolition of offensive warfare.

> The question of territorial disputes between governments and the settlement of these disputes is to all peoples, regardless of race and religion, of primary importance. In the atomic age the responsibility of government is to forestall the danger of a new war . . .
>
> In theory, all governments advocate disarmament; but practical applications have proved unsuccessful . . . Only madmen could want nuclear conflict. In the Soviet Union there are no such people. If they existed, they would be placed in a lunatic asylum. Peoples who dwell on the blood-soaked earth of Europe do not want war . . .
>
> Therefore, the Soviet Union proposes the making of an international treaty by which governments will abolish the use of force in the solution of territorial disputes and frontier problems . . .

This remarkable letter, casting Khrushchev in the unfamiliar role of peace-maker, was slated for sale in my January 14, 1965 auction. A week before the sale the Associated Press carried an article on the letter, commenting also on the great rarity of Khrushchev's signature. The flamboyant dictator, famous for his theatrical outbursts on the United Nations stage, was very firm with the inevitable autograph seekers and seldom granted requests for his signature, possibly in adherence to the Communist policy that all autographs of value belong to

В заключение я хотел бы выразить надежду, что Вы внимательно рассмотрите соображения Советского правительства, изложенные в настоящем послании, и что они найдут у Вас благожелательный отклик. Эти соображения продиктованы интересами мира, стремлением содействовать предотвращению войны.

С уважением

Н.ХРУШЕВ
Председатель Совета
Министров Союза ССР

Last paragraph, with signature, of Khrushchev's letter to Paz Estenssoro.

the state and none may leave the country.

I was quite certain that the letter had officially never left Russian hands and would be claimed by the Communists. And I had my answer all ready. Khrushchev had just been deposed and designated as an "un-person," and I intended to point out to the claimants, if they approached me for the letter, that an un-person could scarcely have written so physical a piece of property as the letter in my possession.

Only a few hours went by after the appearance of the article in the New York papers before my secretary announced that "two very excited gentlemen with unpronouncable Spanish names would like to speak with you about the Khrushchev letter."

I agreed to see them. I was expecting someone, and I was curious to see who the claimant would be.

They were from the Bolivian delegation to the United Nations and their first act was to lay claim to the letter.

"If you do not turn it over to us at once," said the younger of my visitors, "we shall be obliged to go to court to get it."

"What evidence can you present that the letter belongs to you?" I asked. "After all, it may never have been delivered to you by the Russians; or may have been discarded by you after delivery because Paz Estenssoro was deposed; or the vendor may have sold it to me on behalf of your former president."

"On the face of it, the letter belongs to us."

"It does not," I answered. "On the face of it, it belongs to Paz Estenssoro, to whom it was written."

After further discussion, during which I forcefully pointed out the difficulty of their proving ownership, they asked if they could confer together for a few minutes.

I agreed.

They spoke together in Spanish, firing out expletives so rapidly that their speech seemed to have no commas or periods and I was unable to follow what they were saying.

"Could we use your telephone?" asked one.

I told them to go ahead, and I left them in the privacy of my office.

A few minutes later they emerged and asked to resume the discussion.

"We have just talked with Señor Fernando Ortiz, the Bolivian ambassador to the United Nations, and he has agreed that we will not contest the ownership of the letter provided that you will give us the name and address of the man from whom you purchased it."

"What you ask is impossible," I said. "It is considered unethical in my business to furnish such information."

"We believe that someone has been rifling our diplomatic mail pouches and files—perhaps our top secret files —and it obviously must be one of the few persons who has access to them. Unless we can discover who the thief is, every man in our entire embassy will be suspect.

"Put yourself in our place," he went on. "Suppose a thief had stolen an important and confidential letter from your American files in Bolivia—would you not take every possible means to discover him?"

"Your argument carries a great deal of weight," I said. "If an American had violated our secret files, I cannot think of any punishment too severe for him. Still, I feel that I should get the opinion of my attorney."

I telephoned my lawyer, who said: "In view of the circumstances and the accusation of theft, I think you're morally obliged to give the embassy the name and address of the man who sold you the letter. If he's innocent, he can quickly clear himself. If guilty, he should be punished."

After I hung up, I told my Bolivian visitors that my attorney wanted a written release from Señor Ortiz relinquishing all claim to the Khrushchev letter, in return for which I would give them the seller's name and address.

"He cannot sign away a letter of state," said one. "He has no such authority."

"How do I know you will keep your word?"

"Señor Ortiz has authorized us to give *his* word as a gentleman and an ambassador that no claim will be made by us for the letter."

"That is just as satisfactory to me as a written agreement," I said.

When I told them the name of the mysterious vendor they stared at me in wonder. One of them shook his head. "We never heard of him! On top of that, he's got a German name."

"I'm sorry to furnish you with such a puzzle, gentlemen. But I'm sure you have your little ways and means of finding out things."

"Indeed we do, sir!" And I felt certain I detected a sinister note in their reply.

I heard later that for several days an air of mystery and suspicion and intrigue had pervaded the Bolivian embassy. Then the thief was caught.

I never discovered the name of the man who stole this precious letter, but I subsequently learned that he had not been paid for three months prior to the theft and was in dire need of money.

As for the disputed letter of Khrushchev, it was even more fiercely disputed for at auction. After an exciting battle of bidders, it was knocked down to David Kirschenbaum of the Carnegie Book Shop in New York for $1675. This was more than twice as much as was fetched by a pair of Washington and Lincoln letters in the same sale and set a world's record for a letter written by a dictator.

3

THE GREAT ARCHIVES THEFT

Colonel Andrew Barnett of Kansas City did not have a very distinguished script, I thought, as I studied the letter in front of me. Each word was laboriously set down, like the painful effort of a schoolboy. But the colonel's proposition was unusual and appealing. Writing on the letterhead of his shop, "Barnett's Curios," he explained that he had a cache of more than fifty handwritten letters of President Harry S Truman which he wished to swap for letters of earlier Presidents.

Handwritten letters of Truman are extremely rare and valuable, for virtually all of his letters were typed for him by a secretary. I have seen or handled hundreds of letters handwritten by Washington and Lincoln; but I have seen only one handwritten letter of Truman—and that one was not for sale. Thus the colonel's offer was exciting and unusual. Ordinarily I might have questioned his sincerity; but, because his shop was located in Kansas City, where Truman had lived for so many years, I knew it was quite possible for him to have unearthed a group of Truman letters.

So I wrote to Colonel Barnett. After exchanging several letters with him and with his wife, Ruth, I mailed him about $500 worth of rare letters of Andrew Jackson, James Monroe and John Quincy Adams. Colonel Barnett agreed to bring the Truman letters to my New York shop, where I could read them and suggest a fair exchange for the material I had sent him.

But the exchange was hardly what I considered fair. I received no visit from the colonel and no Truman letters. Just silence, from then on.

I wrote to the Barnetts, but my letters came back undelivered. Next I wrote several times to the postal authorities in Kansas City, asking them to investigate the Barnetts. They replied that they were not responsible for personal debts.

Finally, in desperation, I sent a heated letter to the postmaster general in Washington, demanding action. At my insistence, a postal inspector began an inquiry in Kansas City which disclosed the fact that many other dealers and collectors had been similarly swindled by the Barnetts. It seems that I had been lured by the same bait that had snared a whole school of autograph enthusiasts —as well as coin, stamp, and book collectors. And my irate demands had finally sparked a long-overdue inquiry which marked my entry into the most amazing man-hunt in the history of manuscript collecting.

By now I was thoroughly roused, and I vowed that

somehow I would catch up with these two thieves and put them behind bars.

My first encouraging step in that direction came when I met a talented New York postal inspector named Gerard Mailloux, who proved to be an intuitive genius when it came to picking up cold trails.

Working with Arthur Nehrbass, a special agent for the FBI, Mailloux discovered that a number of seemingly unrelated cases, many of them being handled by other postal and FBI operatives, were all linked to the Kansas City swindlers. It seems the Barnetts were wanted by twelve different states, under a dozen different aliases, for a variety of crimes, mostly involving mail thefts of autographs, coins, arrowheads, rare stamps, and Currier and Ives prints.

The man I knew as Colonel Andrew Barnett turned out to be an ex-sailor named Samuel George Matz. He was born in Cleveland, Ohio, in 1918, where he lived in an orphanage until he was eleven. After that he was "farmed out" to a succession of private rural families, where he apparently received room and board in exchange for helping with the farm work. He finished only the ninth grade in school. At seventeen he enlisted in the army but was discharged a few years later because of hyperthyroidism.

In Pocatello, Idaho, when he was 21, he was arrested for lewd cohabitation. Not quite six weeks later he was married to a girl with flaming red hair, Sylvia E. Roewer. The pair moved into her home in Crystal Lake, Illinois,

Inspector George Mailloux.

where she worked as a waitress to support him. He beat her regularly and especially enjoyed slashing off her clothes with a razor.

From here the story becomes confusing because, although there are no records of a divorce, we find that Sam was married again, in January 1948, this time to a woman named Dorothy Dalton. But he soon deserted her to run off with an eighteen-year-old girl from Brooklyn, Vera Carrano. His third marriage was apparently his last, to the woman whom I knew as Ruth Barnett, in 1955.

During his wild series of marital adventures—legal and otherwise—he sired about a dozen children, approximately one for every state where he was later wanted. He abandoned most of them. Those he didn't abandon, he criminally abused. At Pine Bluff, Arkansas, Matz and his last wife, Elizabeth, were arrested for locking their children in a room without food or water.

Matz's landlady in Atlantic City recalled: "Mr. John Adams, the name under which I knew Matz, was a cruel and selfish man. I believe he deliberately starved his children. One afternoon he sat in the yard reading a book and eating a large piece of chocolate cake. His children watched, hungrily, with quiet tears running down their cheeks because they didn't dare cry out loud for fear of a beating. Matz ate the entire piece of cake, then licked the frosting and crumbs from his fingers. I was so upset that I called the children inside and gave them each a sandwich. Judging from the way they gulped them down, almost without chewing, I don't think they had eaten in several days."

During his wife's last pregnancy, about two years before his capture, the FBI was so hot on his trail that Matz decided to play the role of midwife, and he actually delivered her baby without any assistance in their tiny apartment.

This, then, was the man who had operated in Akron, Ohio in 1957, in Springfield, Ohio in 1958, in Baltimore the same year, in Flint, Michigan in 1959, in Kansas City in 1958 and 1959, in Atlantic City in 1960, in Roanoke, Virginia and Evansville, Indiana in 1961.

During the course of these migrations, Sam and Elizabeth Matz had been known as John and Louise Adams (of Adams Art Imports), Wayne and Helen Martin (of the Martin Pen Co.), Dr. J. Webster and Elizabeth Kane, Bradford and Rachel Armstrong, Robert and Linda Benson, Robert J. and Betty Arlene Williams. They also posed as Mr. and Mrs. J. W. Novak and as Mr. and Mrs. Manuel C. Weigel.

When Inspector Mailloux told me about Matz's record, he didn't know, and neither did I, that their biggest victim was the United States Government—bilked out of a half-million dollars worth of rare documents, neatly lifted by Sam and Liz Matz from the National Archives in Washington, D.C. The $500 worth of letters they stole from me no doubt seemed like scraps to them compared with the volumes of priceless letters and documents they sneaked out of the National Archives. But the ease with which they clipped me must have made them drool.

"I have a hunch," confided Mailloux, "that they think you're an easy mark. Chances are they'll come back again to see if they can pick you a little cleaner."

"Have you got a postoffice wanted poster with you?" I asked him.

"We're getting one out now, with examples of their handwriting. I'll send you a copy as soon as it comes off the press."

As a manuscript dealer I have an uncanny memory for handwriting but a very poor recall of faces. I remember a man's signature years after I have forgotten what he looks like. So when the poster arrived, complete with photos and descriptions, I barely glanced at the pictures. But I memorized their handwriting. I resolved that no alias would disguise the Matzes from me if ever I got another letter from them.

Then I put the poster in an envelope on which I wrote, prophetically, "File this where you can find it when I ask for it, as I inevitably will," and gave it to my assistant, Roselle Morse.

On September 28, 1962, while I was at home for lunch, only a few minutes' walk from my shop, she phoned me:

"A woman was just in the shop with three important-looking autographs, including a letter of U. S. Grant. I told her you'd be back to the store in about an hour, so she left the documents with us. She's coming back shortly for your offer."

Then Roselle quipped, "There was something naggingly familiar about her wart-studded face. I think maybe it's Ruth Barnett! I must remember it from the wanted poster Inspector Mailloux gave us. I looked at it quite closely."

"Get out that wanted poster. I'm coming right in to look at it!"

I knew Roselle's memory for faces was accurate, but I wanted to be absolutely certain that we were dealing with Mrs. Barnett before calling in the authorities.

"We've all been looking everywhere for the poster," Roselle apologized on the phone, "but we can't find it. I filed it myself, but I guess I thought it was so important that it deserved a special filing place. So now I just can't remember where I put it!"

I grabbed what I hoped was the jacket to the suit I was wearing and rushed out of the apartment and over to the shop. Roselle and my other two secretaries were still frantically groping through our files in search of the poster when I arrived.

I tried to reach Mailloux. He was out. I thought of phoning the police department, but it seemed pointless since I knew I would have to spend precious time explaining the case to some officer who was completely unfamiliar with it. Finally I decided to call Joe Chapman of the FBI, a special agent in charge of tracking down stolen art works and also a friend of mine. Joe hurried

Post Office Department
Inspection Service
Office of the Inspector in Charge
Philadelphia 1, Pennsylvania

Case No. 22523-F
October 31, 1962.

(Fingerprints and
Classification on
reverse side)

WANTED—FOR MAIL FRAUD

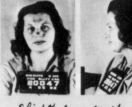

Samuel George Matz
(Applicant's signature)

Mrs. Irene Wilson

SAMUEL GEORGE MATZ: White; age 44, born 1-10-18; 5'8"; 165 lbs.; brown eyes and hair; dark complexion; dresses well; talks big; smokes cigars.

ALIASES: Uses numerous aliases

IRENE ELIZABETH WILSON: White; age about 33; 5'4"; 140 lbs.; brown eyes; brown or black straggly hair; dark complexion; high pitched voice; untidy in personal appearance.

ALIASES: Uses numerous aliases

Since 1957 this couple has used the mails to defraud persons in transactions involving collector items such as rare documents, coins, stamps, guns, etc. They are accompanied in their travels by several of their small children. They rent inexpensive furnished apartments for periods of one to four months and, occasionally, stop at hotels. Between cities they use trains and buses. Within cities they use taxis. They usually open bank accounts in cities visited. They have been indicted for mail fraud. The U. S. Marshal at Newark, N. J., holds warrants for their arrest. If these persons are located please cause their immediate arrest, and notify the undersigned or nearest POSTAL INSPECTOR by telephone or telegraph collect.

Telephone: EVergreen 2-5200, Ext. 418

POSTAL INSPECTOR IN CHARGE
PHILADELPHIA 1, PA.

Samuel and Elizabeth Matz, who successfully eluded the FBI and postal authorities for nearly five years.

over and while we waited for the woman to return, I briefly told him the story and we tried to figure out the best way to handle what was certain to be a touchy situation.

To my relief—because so many crooks seem to have an uncanny intuition that forewarns them when they are walking into a trap—Mrs. Barnett returned shortly after Joe arrived. Joe pretended to be examining some of the framed autographs on the walls while the woman showed me three letters, all authentic.

Ironically, I would have known instantly if this was Ruth Barnett if I could have seen something in her handwriting. But it was certainly frustrating to talk to her and not have any idea if the face was the same as the one on the wanted poster.

One of the letters she offered me was written in 1821 by Andrew Jackson, to Secretary of War John C. Calhoun, complaining bitterly about being forced to borrow money because he had not received his army pay. Another, written in 1866, was from General Ulysses S. Grant to President Andrew Johnson, asking for the pardon of a Confederate soldier, with a note at the bottom in the hand of Johnson, ordering the soldier's release. The third letter, written in 1864 to the provost marshal general, contained information about the disposition of Confederate troops.

I mentally totalled the retail value of the three letters after they had been researched and catalogued. It came to around $600. So I offered $325. She accepted my offer at once, and I said that I would sign a check. Roselle asked to whom she should make out the check and we all heard the name we'd been searching for all afternoon—Mrs. Barbara Palmer.

When Roselle handed her the check, Mrs. Palmer turned to leave. At the same moment—quite by chance, of course—Agent Joe Chapman was just rising to leave. A light rain was falling and Joe, very handsome and debonair, remarked upon this as he gallantly offered her the protection of his umbrella as far as she might need it. She seemed a little rattled by his offer, although she didn't appear actually suspicious. Sensing her indecision, Joe gave her no chance to refuse as he held open the door for her. He turned as he was leaving and gave us a broad, conspiratorial wink. Then he turned up the collar of his tan-colored trenchcoat as he joined Mrs. Palmer, and together they headed into the wind-blown rain in the direction of Fifth Avenue. I watched them for a moment through the big front window as Joe slipped into another identity and engaged Mrs. Palmer in animated conversation. I hoped he would play that part well. In any event, he had certainly made a successful exit, if my wife, who was there pretending to be one of my secretaries, can be considered a valid critic. She told me Joe looked exactly like a Hollywood interpretation of a British secret agent.

I waited at the store for about two hours, impatient to know the outcome of our adventure. At about five o'clock Joe came in, looking a little abashed. I gave him a drink in my private office, and this is the story I heard:

"I walked only as far as the corner (Fifth Avenue at Fifty-third Street) and there she thanked me and said she was meeting someone nearby. She seemed nervous and eager to get rid of me, so I didn't offer to walk farther with her. But I watched as she crossed Fifty-third and walked down to Fifty-second. At the corner a man with a baby carriage—I guessed it was her husband—was waiting for her. They spoke for a moment, and then she strolled off, wheeling the pram.

"I had been walking toward them and trying to decide how to approach, but when 'Mrs. Palmer' walked off my problem was solved. I went up to her husband and introduced myself, saying that I had run into his wife in Hamilton's autograph shop.

" 'Aren't you a Philadelphia antiques dealer?' I asked him. 'I'm sure I've seen you there.'

"Sam admitted that he was, and then he popped a pill of some sort into his mouth. In fact, he was practically dining on pills all the time I was chatting with him.

" 'Say,' I told him, 'I'd be interested in any good autograph letters you run across. Maybe you could sell direct to me, instead of to dealers like Hamilton. That way I could buy cheaper and you could sell for more.'

"Sam said he liked the idea, and we chatted for awhile about autographs and antiques. He even pulled out his wallet, fished out a passport photo of himself and presented it to me.

"By now we were real buddies, but my only problem was that I still did not know whether or not this was the same man who was sought by the FBI. I couldn't arrest him just on suspicion, because I had no evidence that he was wanted—only Roselle's uncertain identification of his wife.

"But I didn't want Sam to get away. Finally I hit upon the idea of asking him to have a drink with me.

" 'Fine,' Sam agreed.

"I told him, 'I'll have to phone my wife and tell her I'll be a bit late for dinner. Would you mind waiting for a few seconds while I call from this store?'

"Sam agreed to wait, so I ducked into a little store right near the corner and called up my office. I found out there was not just one warrant for this man—there were three!

"I rushed outside to arrest him, and guess what. No don't guess—you don't even need to. He was gone!"

I could see that Joe hated to tell me Sam had slipped through his fingers so I didn't criticize him.

"He must have sensed that I was a cop. Or maybe his wife came back while I was on the telephone. She was much more wary than he was, especially since I'm pretty sure he was high from all those pills he was taking— probably some kind of dope."

I told Joe not to worry about it. I would stop payment on the check; and we would consider the whole episode as a fine adventure. At least they wouldn't make any money on this caper! And they didn't dare come back for their documents.

What about those documents? I was reasonably sure

they were stolen. But from whom? I had no way of knowing. Still I was very certain they didn't belong to me, since I hadn't paid for them. I decided to file them until I found the legal owner.

The next morning when I arrived at the store the girls were jubilant. They had found the wanted poster.

I was framing an appropriate reply—something about how wonderful they would think it was if I were to sign this week's salary checks 'just a day late,' when one of my secretaries, who had been out the day before when Mrs. Palmer was in cried:

"Why, that's the woman who was in three weeks ago and sold you a Lincoln signature. Remember, you paid her $100 for it. She told me her name was Barbara Palmer!"

Naturally I remembered buying the signature of Lincoln; but it wasn't until the following morning that it suddenly occurred to me that, if the Matzes had cashed my $100 check, the endorsement would provide the clue to their whereabouts.

I yelled to my assistant, "See if that $100 check cleared and, if so, through what bank!"

She called our bank and found out that they had cashed my check and that it bore the stamp of a Philadelphia bank. I had her phone this information immediately to the postal authorities and the FBI in Philadelphia. The next morning I got a phone call from the FBI in Philadelphia.

I talked to the agent who had been assigned to the case.

"We raced over to the bank the moment we got your call," he told me, "but we arrived just about five minutes too late. The Matzes had already been there. They have an account with the bank, and they took your $325 check in and tried to cash it. But the bank turned them down, because they only had one dollar in their account."

"The bank should have been able to give you their address, anyway," I said.

"They did. And that was our next stop. We had a search warrant; but we didn't want to use it unless we had to, because we were afraid Mrs. Matz might be at home and Sam out, or vice versa. So we decided the best thing to do was wait for one or both of them to come or go. I took the first shift.

"I had been waiting for several hours when suddenly I noticed a creepy looking guy who seemed to be shadowing me. I started watching him out of the corner of my eye, and I could see that he was edging closer and closer to the Matz apartment building. As you can imagine, I'm a trained observer. And the longer I watched this man, the more certain I was that I had better have a talk with him, and, if necessary, place him under arrest.

"So I waited for the right moment, and then I crept up on him and grabbed his arm:

" 'FBI!' I cried, and flipped open my wallet with my identification.

"Before I could stop him his hand went inside his coat and came out holding something shiny.

" 'United States postal inspector!' " he said, flashing his badge. I must have looked just as startled for a moment as he had a second earlier. But when the comedy of the situation hit us, we both burst into laughter. He told me that I had looked just as suspicious to him as he had to me, as we stood there furtively eyeing one another, like two actors in a bad melodrama.

"Finally, though, we decided to put our credentials to more serious work. We both had search warrants, and it was time to use them. When we knocked at the Matzes' door we got no answer. I demanded loudly that they let us in and the inspector shouted through the door that we were police officers. Still we got no answer so we kicked in the door. They were gone!

"And they had left in a great hurry. Half of their belongings were strewn all over the floor—we even found syringes and other equipment for taking dope. They must have got out of the apartment and out of Philadelphia within half an hour after the bank refused to cash that check."

I chatted for a few more minutes with the agent, and he said he would telephone me if he heard of any important developments in the case. But it was months before I was to hear anything more about the Matzes.

Then, one afternoon, I had a visit from an old friend, Colonel Walter Pforzheimer of Washington, D.C., an autograph collector who specializes in espionage material. As we sat in my office with a drink, he told me about a recent experience:

"I got a phone call from a small book store in Washington. The owner told me he had just bought a collection of letters and documents about spies during the Civil War. He wanted to know if I was interested in buying them. I was, as you can imagine; and I got to his place as fast as I could.

"He had a remarkable collection of secret letters—so interesting and valuable that they really belonged in an institution or library. And he only wanted $200 for the entire group. So I bought it, of course; and I could hardly wait to show off the collection to a friend of mine who's writing a history of espionage during the Civil War. But after I opened the carton and showed him only a couple of papers, he suddenly began pulling them out one after another and reading them with disbelief. 'My God, Walt, I photographed these identical documents not more than a month ago in the National Archives!'

"Naturally I was horrified," Pforzheimer went on, "and I called the dealer. He was pretty scared himself—I don't think he had any idea where they'd come from— and he gave me back my money. I turned the material over to Wayne C. Grover, the chief archivist. Grover was flabbergasted. He didn't even know they'd been stolen!

"So, anyway, watch out, Charlie! There may be some more espionage stuff from the National Archives still on the market. The FBI hasn't been able to get any line at all on the thieves."

"Can you give me a more specific idea of what to look for?" I asked him.

"All I can tell you is that many of the documents were signed by a Captain McEntee."

Captain McEntee. I had seen that name, I was sure.

"Just a minute, Walter," I said, and got up from my chair. "That name sounds familiar. Let me look in the file here." And I went to the drawer where Roselle had put the letters I bought from Sam and Elizabeth Matz. I was right. One of the letters was signed by Captain McEntee!

Walter telephoned the National Archives for me, and they asked me to send photostats, so that they could see if the documents really were from their collection. I immediately had the photostats made, and mailed them out. Then I waited for some word from the Archives, letting me know what I should do with the letters. But for almost a year I got no acknowledgment of the photostats.

Then one afternoon I got a telephone call from Stephen Kaufman, assistant United States attorney in New York, asking me formally for the return of the documents to the National Archives. I sent back the letters by registered mail.

When the story of the National Archives theft broke on the front page of *The New York Times* the next day, the search for Sam and Elizabeth Matz was stepped up.

They had picked the wrong pocket this time. Uncle Sam may have a lot of pockets, but he nevertheless doesn't like it when one of them is looted.

How the Matzes had managed to elude arrest is difficult to understand. They should have been easy to spot. In spite of all the babies they had abandoned, they still had to travel with five other children, one of whom was only an infant in a perambulator. And their photographs, with descriptions, adorned the walls of countless post offices—Sam, as he was projected by the wanted posters, "dresses well, talks big, smokes cigars." Liz was described as having "a high-pitched voice" and being "untidy in personal appearance." My wife, who had talked to her in the shop, told me that this was an understatement. "She was very messy looking and seemed rather beaten and pathetic."

One explanation for the Matzes' success at dodging the law was that they had doctored their looks. Sam had grown a shaggy mustache; and Liz's warts had almost disappeared—as a result of electrolysis, we learned later.

Still, they seemed to slip in and out of the hands of the law almost as if they were charmed. For example, only a few weeks before their final capture, an off-duty cop in Cincinnati was sitting in a drug store when he noticed a man and woman with a young girl. He felt they looked a little suspicious; and, from force of habit, his eyes followed them as they walked among the counters. As he watched, the man suddenly reached down, grabbed three bottles of expensive hair tonic and slipped them into a shopping bag the child was holding.

The policeman arrested the shoplifters. Sam was held for $300 bail, but Elizabeth was released without bail to care for their children. The next day she came to see her husband, and she brought with her $250. Sam managed to produce the additional fifty dollars, and he was set free to await trial. By the time the couple was identified as Samuel and Elizabeth Matz, two of the most-wanted fugitives in the nation, the vagabond family had vanished.

The elusive trail of the Matzes, which invariably dead-ended in hastily abandoned rooming houses or hotels, finally led to Detroit where detectives, with the aid of James Babcock, an alert archivist from the Detroit Public Library, set a trap for the ghostlike pair.

Babcock had been fortunate in buying important historic documents for bargain prices from a woman who gave her name as Mrs. R. McClaferty. The last time Mrs. McClaferty brought in some documents for his offer, he asked her to wait in his office while he went to seek approval for his final purchase from Charles Mohrhardt, associate director of the library. When Babcock entered Mohrhardt's office, he was astonished to find the director in an argument with Dr. McClaferty, who was insisting upon the use of restricted documents for his research. Babcock suddenly had a hunch that Dr. McClaferty and his research project—and even his wife who was waiting in Babcock's office—just weren't authentic. He felt that he should warn his superior and he confided to Mohr-hardt that there was something "very suspicious about the whole deal."

The librarians took a quick inventory of the institution's historical documents. They discovered that many valuable papers, including numerous maps, had disappeared from the shelves, but they could find no withdrawal slips for the missing pieces. They decided to call in the FBI.

Library officials, working with the FBI, persuaded Mrs. McClaferty to return with more documents; and they promised Dr. McClaferty that he would be granted access to restricted areas. Then, after drawing the couple into this double trap, the FBI agents trailed them to their apartment.

Armed with a search warrant, the agents entered the Matzes' apartment and placed them under arrest. They looked through the flat, where they found seven suitcases bulging with important historical papers. There were letters by Lincoln, Andrew Jackson, Woodrow Wilson, Franklin D. Roosevelt, Dwight D. Eisenhower and John F. Kennedy. And there were more than fifty letters of President James Monroe. Among the rarities was a handwritten note of Lincoln, dated April 14, 1865, the day of his murder.

A later search by the FBI turned up ten more cartons of stolen documents. One expert evaluated the looted collection at more than half-a-million dollars—most of it heisted from the National Archives, a huge building which houses the precious manuscript treasures of our country, from the Declaration of Independence and Constitution to the most recent law signed by the President.

Under the name of Dr. Robert Bradford Murphy, Sam Matz, with his wife, who posed as his assistant, had visited the National Archives frequently in the fall of 1962. They pretended to be at work on an important research project for the University of Chicago, and Liz Matz evidently slipped manuscripts into her handbag during each visit. Briefcases and parcels are usually examined at the door as a researcher leaves the building, but a woman's purse is never examined for fear of invading her privacy. So, taking advantage of the library's courtesy, Sam and Elizabeth Matz pulled off the first and only recorded theft from the National Archives—and in a manner so ludicrously naïve that it was at the same time diabolically clever.

In prison, held on $40,000 bail, Matz continued to devour pills. Then he demanded treatment for a heart condition, and for medical reasons he was finally transferred to the federal prison at Milan, Michigan.

During their trial in 1964 the Matzes maintained an arrogant composure. Matz insisted upon acting as his own lawyer, and summoned witnesses whom he had defrauded or attempted to defraud. Among his curious choices was the prominent New York dealer, Mary A. Benjamin, whose testimony the court found very damaging to Matz. He also tried to summon me but the trial

45

was held in Detroit and I have a pathological aversion to travel for any other than a worthy cause—and I didn't consider the Matzes' cause to be a worthy one. So, with the assistance of a black trench coat and sunglasses, and the unfamiliar adornment of a straw hat which my wife picked out for the occasion, I managed to elude the bailiff who made many unannounced visits to both my shop and my apartment.

It was just as well. I would have appeared as a witness if I had felt there was even the smallest doubt that the Matzes would not be convicted. But the trial lasted only a few days. And in those few days the jury was confronted with so many gruesome accounts of Sam and Elizabeth's treatment of their children and one another, not to speak of the countless people they coldly defrauded, that their captive audience of twelve took very little time to reach a "guilty" decision.

In passing a sentence of ten years in prison on both Sam and his wife, the judge expressed a vehement personal conviction: "In all my years on the bench, I have never seen such a despicable pair as you two!"

I guess I will have to agree with that judge. But then, perhaps my condemnation of Sam Matz is almost an impertinence. After all, he was, for a brief period, the custodian of the most important privately owned autograph collection in the world.

4

PREXIES BY PROXY

President Lyndon B. Johnson's secretary, Juanita Roberts, gasped with indignation over my assertion that the President had permitted a secretary to sign an executive order for him. "Ask Mr. Hamilton," she said heatedly to a reporter, "when he has witnessed a Presidential signature. As far as I know he has never done so. I would like that gentleman to pay a visit to the Archives and see the bills and pick the one he thinks is a fake because every single one was signed by Lyndon Johnson."

It is certainly true that I have never seen Johnson write his name (nor have I seen Washington or Lincoln write theirs.) But forty years in the autograph field have given me a sensitivity to scrawls, leaving me unimpressed even by the further substantiating claim of Lee White, special counsel to President Johnson, who added: "The President does not allow anyone else to sign executive orders for him. Even the most routine ones designating American Baseball Week or a Mother's Day proclamation all are signed personally by him. There is just no question about it."

No question? It is an aide's job to say what the President wants him to say. But I am self-employed and thus enjoy a freedom of speech not possible to those on the President's staff. I am sure they have often seen him scribble his name, but I should like to offer the suggestion that the next time they witness this act they be a little more observant. They will find that Johnson writes not at all like the first example given on the facsimile page here, for this signature, affixed to an executive order, is definitely not in the President's hand. Virtually every letter in this halting and puerile fake differs from his vigorous signature. This same proxy imitation, incidentally, is very common and is found in many collections of young people who solicit autographs from President Johnson.

On the other hand, the authentic signatures of Johnson, illustrated on the same page, are quite scarce. Although I have examined hundreds of "signed" photographs and White House cards of Johnson, I have yet to find one which, in my opinion, bore a genuine signature. Yet nearly all of them are accompanied by letters of secretaries testifying to their authenticity.

It is a cruel blow to a collector to find that he has been "taken" by The White House, and that his treasured signature was signed, not by the President, but by a secretary or a robot.

Even a professional graphologist was drawn into this trap. I was vastly amused to read in a recent book on

THREE "PREXY BY PROXY" SIGNATURES
OF LYNDON B. JOHNSON

Top: A "prexy by proxy" signature affixed by a ghost penman to an executive order announcing official mourning for Sir Winston Churchill; Lower left: Another type of proxy signature from a White House letter dated February 23, 1965, to Professor Joseph Kaplan of U.C.L.A.; Lower right: A third proxy signature of Johnson, written on a first-day cover honoring American Flag Day, postmarked July 4, 1957.

Vice President of the United States and
President of the Senate.

AUTHENTIC SIGNATURES OF JOHNSON
AS VICE-PRESIDENT AND PRESIDENT

Three authentic signatures of Johnson, all taken from official documents, show the wide variance in his hand. Compared with the imitations illustrated above, Johnson's own signature is bold and virile. Notice that when he wishes, the President can write a very clear schoolmaster's hand.

graphology an analysis of a crude secretarial imitation of Johnson's signature—which the graphologist mistakenly believed was that of the President: "Alert, intelligent, shrewd, politically aware, forceful but willing to compromise"—heaps of glowing adjectives were piled high upon the menial clerk whose feeble imitation inspired the graphologist. After I read it all, I commented: "Great Scott! Johnson's pen-clerk should be President. If graphology is right, we have the wrong man in The White House!"

The rash of Presidential proxies really began with Old Hickory, back in 1834. Before the era of that doughty soldier, all Presidents had personally assumed the burden of signing the countless hundreds of routine documents which crossed their desk each week—landgrants, ship's papers, military and civil appointments, routine or important letters. It was a quill-splitting job even in the days of Washington, but by the time of Andrew Jackson the mere signing of the President's name must have required an hour or two each morning.

One day in 1834 Andrew Jackson rebelled. Never a facile penman, he faced an enemy cannon with more composure than an inkwell and quill; and he must have reached his important decision as he confronted the daily Pike's Peak of documents awaiting his signature. Doubtless he summoned his private secretary, Andrew J. Donelson, and said: "In the future, you will write my name on all landgrants. I will continue to sign personally all other official documents."

From 1835 on, no President placed his personal signature on landgrants. Successors of Old Hickory did, however, maintain the tradition of signing ship's papers and military appointments. Zachary Taylor's secretary occasionally franked a letter for him, but until Lincoln's time, virtually every official document, except for landgrants, bore the authentic scrawl of the President.

The demands of conducting a war ate so heavily into Lincoln's time that he gave up the signing of ship's papers (only a few bearing his signature exist), but he did continue to place his name on innumerable military, naval and civil commissions. His successor, Andrew Johnson, put an end to this and other time-consuming tasks by using a metal stamp to sign most commissions and appointments. These may readily be recognized by collectors because the ink is very black and often slightly smudged. Johnson's franking signature, as President, was occasionally signed for him by his son, who also sometimes wrote and signed letters for his famous father. The son's penmanship is much finer and more regular.

Oddly, despite the crushing workload of the Presidency, the Chief Executives from Grant to Wilson insisted upon signing all commissions and appointments, even those for West Point cadets, army shavetails, or naval ensigns. Theodore Roosevelt employed a secretary who imitated his signature with modest skill, but that was during the periods before and after his incumbency. As President, he signed personally all of the documents which bear his signature. The first of his successors to introduce again the printed signature was Woodrow Wilson, and his policy was followed by most Chief Executives of the modern era.

During the period when he was considered as a possible Presidential candidate and while he was running for office, Warren G. Harding delegated to his secretary,

(Top) Secretarial signature of Warren G. Harding, signed for him by George B. Christian; (Bottom) Authentic signature of Warren G. Harding.

George B. Christian, the signing of his name to routine correspondence. In a recent issue of "The Collector," the distinguished dealer, Mary A. Benjamin, discussed at length the original signature of Harding and the imitation by Christian. If you study the two signatures carefully, you will find many differences, the most conspicuous of which are the middle initial *G*, the capital *H*, and the terminal *g* on Harding.

When Harding entered The White House, Christian ceased to sign his name for him.

52

On very rare occasions, Coolidge and Hoover employed secretaries to sign their names, but never while President. Franklin D. Roosevelt used no less than seven

Authentic signature of Franklin D. Roosevelt, 1932 (top). The secretarial signature that fooled an expert, 1932 (bottom). The bottom example, one of the most skilled imitations of Roosevelt's signature, signed only to letters written during his 1932 Presidential campaign, passed current as an authentic signature of F.D.R. for many years. A careful comparison with the authentic signature of the same period will, however, reveal that every single letter in the proxy signature is different from F.D.R.'s own scrawl.

different proxy signers during the course of his career, but, as Chief Executive, he signed personally every document which required his signature and when he complied with a request for his autograph, he invariably signed with his own hand. Although politically astute and sometimes ruthless, he disliked any sort of deception and had recourse to secretarial signatures only when the burden of work became almost insupportable.

Except during a brief period as senator, Harry S Truman has always insisted upon signing his own mail personally. Even in retirement (except very recently,

Sincerely yours,

Secretarial signature of Harry S Truman signed in 1967.

since 1967) he has continued to put his personal signature on every letter he dictates.

During his Presidential campaign, General Dwight D. Eisenhower employed two secretaries to sign routine mail for him (1952); examples of both imitations are illustrated in my book, *Collecting Autographs and Manuscripts*. As President, he signed personally all letters and important official papers. Because of illness since his retirement, Eisenhower has been forced to turn most of his correspondence over to secretaries and to decline to furnish his autograph to applicants. Recently (1966), however, he has been sending out photographs bearing a rather inept proxy imitation, distinguished for its lack of the middle initial *E*. The specimen illustrated here was furnished to me by Paul K. Carr, the Rockville, Maryland collector, and I have been shown other examples of the same fabrication by the distinguished Brookline, Massachusetts dealer, Paul C. Richards.

With the era of John F. Kennedy, we move into a period of amazing official audacity, in which it has become common practice for The White House to warrant as

Secretarial signature of Dwight D. Eisenhower signed in 1967. It can readily be identified by the lack of a middle initial.

genuine all sorts of proxy signatures and even robot imitations. Kennedy established the policy of sending out secretarial imitations of his signature to applicants, accompanied by letters of his aides stating that "the President was pleased to sign this photograph for you" or "I called your request to the attention of the President, and he was delighted to write his name in your book." This incredible deception goes even further. Kennedy allowed his secretary, Evelyn Lincoln, to sign personally some of his mail written on White House stationery. Examples of Mrs. Lincoln's proxy signature, together with thirteen other secretarial signatures of Kennedy, are illustrated in my book, *The Robot that Helped to Make a President.*

With the examples set by Presidents Kennedy and Lyndon B. Johnson, it is little wonder that other distinguished personalities of our era resort to the same policy. Mrs. Kennedy, for example. Her own signature is so delicate and beautiful, reflecting the personality that most Americans love and are fascinated by, that it seems al-

Top: Two secretarial signatures of Jacqueline Kennedy; Bottom: Authentic signature of Mrs. Kennedy.

most ridiculous to place it beside the pedestrian imitations of her secretaries. Even when I present evidence to support my views, most owners of Mrs. Kennedy letters *insist* that the noble lady signed personally for them. Early in 1964, I declined to buy a letter of Mrs. Kennedy bearing an obvious secretarial signature, and the owner came back with:

"I wrote to Miss Tuckerman [Jacqueline Kennedy's social secretary], saying that my 'friends' said the signature was not an original, and asked her if Jacqueline had actually signed the letter. At that time the First Lady was carrying the baby who died at birth in August and I am sure she passed by Miss Tuckerman's White House office many times a day . . . I received the following letter signed by one of Miss Tuckerman's secretaries . . . : 'Miss Tuckerman has asked me to answer your letter of January 16th, as the mail prevents her from answering everyone personally. She remembers your presentation of the volume . . . and says that the signature in question is that of Mrs. Kennedy.'

"It looks therefore that your judgment in this particular case was rather inexpert . . ."

If owners of Mrs. Kennedy letters are volatile, how much more easily inflamed are collectors of other modern heroes! To take only one example: Albert Schweitzer. During the last thirty-five or forty years of his life, Schweitzer, who had suffered from writer's cramp from the age of twenty-five, employed a secretary who imitated with extraordinary skill not only his signature, but his handwriting. For nearly a decade I had heard vague rumors that Schweitzer seldom—indeed, almost never—signed any letters or papers. His constant companion and secretary not only assumed the burden of writing to autograph collectors, sending letters, signed photos, pen-drawn maps, souvenirs of all kinds, but even took care of intimate and important correspondence for him.

How then could I discover the *real* signature of Dr. Schweitzer?

Quite by accident I acquired a letter of Dr. Schweitzer, penned in blue ink and signed in red ink, in which he explained to an old friend that because of illness he was dictating the letter. The signature was quite remarkable, with an umbrella-like flourish across the final four letters of his name. Could this be the elusive, actual signature of the great humanitarian?

A few months later, I purchased a letter of Schweitzer written early in the 1920's, shortly before he acquired the amanuensis who was to be the plague of historians and collectors. Again, the umbrella flourish.

Authentic handwriting and signature of Albert Schweitzer, showing his method of writing the terminal "tzer" of his signature.

Finally I achieved my goal—a letter partly in the hand of his secretary and partly in the hand of Schweitzer. She had penned his name without the umbrella, like the scores of other Schweitzer signatures on the market, and he had pitched over his scrawl a perfect *parapluie*.

Although not all of my confreres agree with me, I feel almost certain that the very rare signature of Schweitzer can only be identified as genuine, beyond question, if it bears the umbrella flourish.

As we get further away from the old days when a man's signature was his bond, we can expect more and more proxy scrawls on letters and documents. But such impositions and deceptions only make the chase more exciting and add piquancy to the historian's task.

5

THE ROBOT THAT WORKS
FOR THE PRESIDENT

Picture a great, faceless robot that clutches a fountain pen in fingers of steel. At the press of a pedal, it comes to life, tirelessly writing signature after signature, each with its own tiny variations.

This is the amazing automaton which for the past six years has taken over the human function of writing the signature of the President of the United States. It wrote the name *John F. Kennedy* thousands of times and, with the mere replacement of a signature matrix, requiring only a few seconds, it was ready to scrawl the signature of his successor, *Lyndon B. Johnson.*

No secret weapon was ever more assiduously guarded, and White House aides vehemently deny that the robot exists. "There is no machine," insisted Pierre Salinger, press secretary to Kennedy, to which statement Johnson aides have added their amens.

But today the Autopen 50, which is the trade name for the President's robot, is so widely used that many statesmen seldom take the pen from its hands. Robot signatures have been ruled legal. It is a horrifying thought, that a steel monster can sign the President's name so perfectly that it would pass as authentic even under the closest scrutiny. Such a robot could sign a document which might plunge the nation into war, or act in the President's place if he were indisposed or if he died and the news were withheld. It can't happen here? Perhaps not, but the possibility exists so long as the robot exists.

The Autopen 50, or robot, now being used by the President consists of a desk-like structure in which is placed a complicated steel mechanism, terminating in the claws which grip a fountain pen. A signature matrix, which resembles a crudely carved boomerang, is fitted on a large rotating disk. When the machine is started, the disk rotates, and the wavy markings on the matrix activate the pen, much in the same manner as the track in a phonograph record. The robot can write as many as three thousand signatures a day.

To start the machine, the operator presses a foot-pedal, leaving his hands free to feed in letters or documents or photographs for signature. The robot can also be placed on automatic, and will continue to sign at brief intervals as fast as the operator can push letters under the pen. There is a lighted glass disk directly beneath the pen, and before using any signature pattern, the operator allows the pen to write on the glass. This temporary signature reflects through the paper and acts as a guide for placing each letter in exactly the right spot.

The Autopen 50 is top secret wherever it is used and no outsiders are ever permitted to see it. When I was

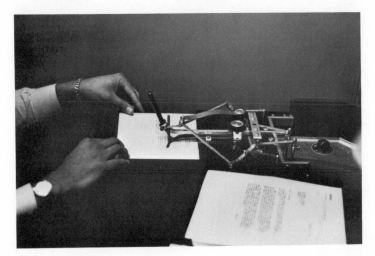

Photo by Roy Schatt

Feeding a letter into the Autopen.

writing my book, *The Robot that Helped to Make a President*, the story of how Kennedy used the Autopen, I pulled every string, resorted to every plea in order to have a look at this remarkable machine. I approached celebrities and executives. I wrote dozens of pleading letters. And after four or five months of hard searching, I had got exactly nowhere.

Finally from The Chase Manhattan Bank I got a tip

that there was a certain large insurance company in New York which had an Autopen 50. Our executive vice president, H. Keith Thompson, Jr., had worked for this company when a young man. He approached the vice president of the insurance company, explaining that we were interested in viewing the machine, and had been referred to him by Mr. DeShazo, the reputed inventor.

"Certainly," said the insurance executive. "And when would you like to take a look at it?"

Keith made an appointment for himself and "several friends." There were four of us, all guilt-stricken over our deception and looking very furtive, who showed up in the vice president's office. Keith was jovial, full of reminiscences of old days with the firm; Roy Schatt, our photographer, carried his camera and tripod jauntily, like a cane, with about as innocent an air as a poacher; my wife, Diane, was repentent even before we started out; and I felt like a naughty schoolboy. Not in years had I used any such ruse. But it was absolutely vital that I have a view of this elusive robot in operation.

"I have a hunch we're going to get pitched out when I take the first picture," whispered Roy.

"Be very casual about it," I whispered back. "And, for heaven's sake, don't look professional. Be sure to bumble around like an amateur."

Accompanied by the insurance company vice president, who was extremely affable and pleasant, discussing "our mutual friend, Mr. DeShazo," we took the elevator to another floor where, after a lengthy stroll through mountains of files, we reached the robot. An operator was there to show us how it worked.

"I'll just take a couple of snapshots as refreshers for when we get back," said Roy, setting up his camera equipment.

"Why don't you try and see if you can operate the Autopen?" I said to Diane. She sat down at the machine and began to work it. Flashbulbs were popping as Roy worked frantically.

"We don't like to make an investment without really looking over what we buy," explained Keith.

"I understand perfectly," said the insurance executive, but with a puzzled look on his face while he watched Roy taking photo after photo.

As I studied the machine, a feeling of horror came over me. It was so much more efficient, so much swifter than any human. I watched it sign letter after letter, each with a perfect signature. Then I asked the operator: "Doesn't the signature pattern on the matrix ever wear out?"

"Oddly, no." The operator lifted the matrix out of the machine. "See how light it is, all plastic. It actually outlasts these metal posts between which it passes in activating the pen. When the posts get worn on one side, and the signature tends to level out, we simply turn them around and use the other side. If we kept using the posts indefinitely, the signature would ultimately become nothing more than a straight line. But when both sides of the

Photo by Roy Schatt; posed by Diane Hamilton

Writing a signature with the Autopen.

post are worn out, we get new ones. We only replace the matrix if it accidentally gets chipped.

"What are these wavy lines in the matrix?"

"As the matrix passes through the little metal posts, each curve affects the movement of the pen. And these humps on top of the matrix lift the pen up, so as to separate the first from the last name, or dot an *i*."

The operator fitted another matrix into the machine, placing it on the large flat circular wheel, then pressed the starting switch. He showed how the signature was written as the wheel rotated, passing the matrix between the two posts, with a pause until the matrix completed a full rotation and returned for another signature. "Watch," he said. "I will duplicate the job of the matrix with my hand." He wiggled the two posts, producing a wild scribble on the paper. "If I practised for many years, I might be able to write a word or two."

"Can you use any sort of pen?"

"Yes; right now I'm using an Esterbrook. But even a pencil will sign as well. He took out the Esterbrook and fitted a ballpoint pen into the circular metal claw, tightening a screw to secure it. This time the pen signed with a spidery scrawl, with open *o*'s not visible in the Esterbrook signature.

"And if," continued the operator, "I sigh or breathe deeply while the robot is writing, it will affect the signature. If I sign with the machine working at top speed, the *o*'s and *e*'s and *a*'s tend to fill with ink. Or if the pen is fastened in the holder too low, there may be an extra flourish in the signature. Or too high, whole letters may disappear. Definitely this machine has got a mind of its own."

After the demonstration was over, we four guilty ones skulked out into the street. A light but rather depressing rain was falling. I was enormously pleased that I had at last observed the robot at work, but at the same time there was a doubt in my mind about the propriety of my act in posing as a possible buyer of the machine.

Recently a collector asked me: "How can you tell a robot signature from a genuine one?"

"You can't," I told him, "unless you have other examples of the same robot pattern. Kennedy used seven different robot patterns. If you take two signatures of the same pattern and hold them up to the light, they will superimpose, with certain slight variations. When the pen is lifted up by the robot, there may sometimes be a variation in the space before it is set down, so that you will have to superimpose the first name and the second name separately, because of the variant gap between them."

At present, I know of only three different robot signatures of Lyndon B. Johnson. But it is interesting to note that his wife also has her matrix, so that she will not have to go to the trouble of signing her name for collectors who request it.

Not long ago, on a television program, I commented on the fact that both John F. Kennedy and Lyndon B. Johnson used secretaries or robots to sign autographs, yet accompanied such fakes with authenticating letters by their aides.

"What difference does it really make?" asked the man who was interviewing me. "It saves the President and

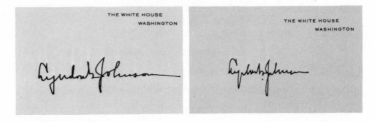

Three robot signatures of President Lyndon B. Johnson. Two have been used for signing White House cards, sent out with an authenticating letter of Juanita D. Roberts, personal secretary to the President.

First Lady a lot of time, and most collectors never know that they are fooled."

"I am very old-fashioned," I answered. "I still believe that the President should set an example of honesty for every boy and girl in the nation."

Perhaps, since the President uses an Autopen, we can scarcely criticize the hundreds of others who send out such fraudulent autographs to collectors, or who use a machine to sign their mail. Such public figures as Robert

F. Kennedy, Richard Nixon and Nelson Rockefeller have doubtless almost forgotten how to write their names, since they have a robot to do it for them.

Both the American and Russian astronauts use an automaton to sign autographs for collectors. One wonders if they are spacemen or robots—or perhaps both! I

Robot signature of Lady Bird Johnson, sent to a collector with a letter signed "Bess Abell, Social Secretary," stating that Mrs. Johnson was "happy to comply with your autograph request."

once saw eighteen postcard photographs of the first Russian spacewoman, all signed in pen and ink with identical signatures.

Possibly the time is coming when handwriting will no longer be necessary. Not long ago I received a letter from David Battan, the Fresno, California, autograph dealer, in which he noted:

"This evening I had a very interesting conversation with an individual who has worked in Senator Robert F. Kennedy's office and Vice President Humphrey's office . . .

"It is well known that Senator Kennedy and Vice President Humphrey use the Autopen. However, my source informed me that there is a new machine in use in both the Senator's office and the Vice President's office which can inscribe material to a specific individual. He told me there is a plate (matrix) made up 'with best wishes/Robert Kennedy' and by typing out the name of an individual the machine can reproduce Kennedy's

First-day cover of Project Mercury, signed by the first seven astronauts, probably with robot signatures. The signatures of Donald K. Slayton, Gus Grissom, Gordon Cooper, and Walter Schirra I have positively identified as signed by Autopen.

handwriting with the name of the person. He said the machine can select any letter of the alphabet in Kennedy's handwriting. When requests are made for personal inscriptions this device is used. He informed me that Hubert Humphrey also uses this device.

"He further informed me that Kennedy and Humphrey do not respond to autograph requests. He has become a close friend of Kennedy and said Kennedy told him he has had to resort to the use of the Autopen although he really does not approve of this method; but he feels it is too late to change the procedure now as it makes his job much easier. I understand that secretaries

Sincerely,

Robert F. Kennedy

Robert F. Kennedy

Widely used robot signature of Robert F. Kennedy.

sign his name on important letters although he may dictate the letters. This individual was even taught how to sign Kennedy's name. His job was to open mail and operate the Autopen for Kennedy.

"The use of the device which inscribes material in Kennedy's hand is very confidential and persons working in the office are not authorized to discuss its use . . .

"I was also told that The White House has fourteen Autopens.

"I feel very strongly towards a policy being established for the use of any robot device and identification of any material so signed. It will be an increasing problem to collectors in the future and the consequences of its use could be serious."

71

Many historians and scholars share David Battan's concern. Recently collector Paul K. Carr sent me some correspondence with Senator Daniel Brewster and L. Quincy Mumford, Librarian of Congress. In response to probing by Carr, transmitted to him by Senator Brewster, Mumford wrote:

"Mechanisms such as the Autopen have become administrative necessities for certain men in public life whose official correspondence is especially voluminous. Documents known to be signed mechanically have relatively little value for an autograph collector, of course, and the impetus for distinguishing authentic personal signatures from mechanically produced cases has come from collectors and dealers in autographs.

"For historical purposes, however, the public official is responsible for utterances which he has authorized to be signed with his name whether or not he holds the pen. The situation is analogous to the practice of having letters drafted for one's signature. The person who signs a document assumes responsibility for its contents and entitles historians to conclude that it represents his own thinking or that of his staff to which he gives assent. Certainly a handwritten private memorandum would have historical authenticity surpassing that of other forms of documentation, but less personal documents, if authorized, are valid objects of historical study . . ."

I have the distinct feeling that Mr. Mumford knows very little about autograph collectors. In the first place, the *contents* of a letter or document, not the signature, are of paramount importance to all those who collect historic documents. A letter of John F. Kennedy, signed with a robot or secretarial signature, may easily fetch several hundred dollars because of significant contents. In his letter to Senator Brewster, Carr mentioned a letter of Kennedy, signed by robot, in which Kennedy gave the reasons why he would not vote for the confirmation of Lewis Strauss to be Eisenhower's secretary of commerce. I have thus far seen four such identical letters, all signed by robot and doubtless written by a robotyper.

Was the original composed or dictated by Kennedy? Or was it some hireling who put into the missive his own thoughts and ideas? If the thoughts were Kennedy's, and Mr. Mumford has no reason other than surmise to say they were, then the letter definitely has value to a collector.

But, a hundred years hence, who will know which letters were composed by the senders? Consider the problems we face now with the famous letter to Mrs. Bixby, consoling her on the death of five sons in battle, presumably written by Lincoln, but sometimes attributed to John Hay. The original—if it ever existed—is now lost. Mr. Mumford may claim it is not important whether or not Lincoln wrote the letter, so long as we know it expresses his ideas. To me it makes a great difference. I would like to know whether the wording of the letter is Lincoln's or Hay's. And, in the absence of a Lincoln signature at the end of the letter, we may never know.

LITERARY LICENSE

The traditions of literary license permit even the least talented to borrow a phrase or a word from great men of letters. But there are those who go beyond such pilferage, who would borrow the man himself, his fame, his signature, even his penned masterpieces. And what scrawls they cannot borrow or steal—they invent.

Strangely, the creative talents of forgers and literary knaves almost match, in a way wholly debased, the achievements of the very authors whose genius they seek to plunder. And because such rogues are the most skilled of literary criminals, their lives and "achievements" are perennially fascinating.

6

LORD BYRON'S "BASTARD SON"

There is no record of the impact that Major Byron had on the ladies. If he was anything like his namesake it must have been cataclysmic. But this self-proclaimed bastard offspring of Lord Byron, *alias* Major George Gordon Byron, *alias* Monsieur Memoir, and *alias* De Gibler (probably his real name) certainly set the world of literary scholarship on its ear. He left behind him a legacy of forged Byron and Shelley letters which continue to perplex and plague collectors and students. Even now in halls of alleged learning there are fierce debates about the authenticity of certain letters which may or may not be in the hand of Lord Byron. For De Gibler— let us call him Major Byron since it costs us nothing to accord him a valueless title—was a forger both artful and articulate who studied and then beautifully counterfeited the flamboyant style of the great Romantic poet. If Major Byron errs in dates and places in his forgeries, he makes up for it with a literary skill so convincing that we have half a mind to overlook the mistakes and credit the production to the great lord.

In the annals of infamy, Major Byron stands out as the only forger who could not merely imitate the style of his subject with consummate skill but could copy his handwriting with even more consummate skill. And his genius went further. With amazing, almost diabolic ingenuity, he fabricated early postmarks on the covers of his forgeries.

Although Major Byron's misdeeds are well known to literary scholars, his biography is lamentably vague. He claimed to own a farm in Wilkes-Barre, Pennsylvania, and another on the Hudson River, about thirty-two miles from New York. Still, he was a skilled beggar, and adroitly solicited funds from John Murray, Byron's publisher, as well as from Mary Shelley and other notables. For a time he lived in New York, where he ran up so many bills that he finally fled to Cleveland. One of his creditors was a bootmaker who had given him credit under the alias of "Major George Gordon Byron of the British Army." While he was in Cleveland, the major apparently spent most of his time writing begging letters to celebrities and speculating unsuccessfully in real estate.

In March, 1886, *The American Antiquarian* printed a capsule account of Major Byron's residence in New York: "His office at No. 40 Broadway, where he professed to do business, was rather a mythical one, he having simply permission to use part of a room there. He made a show of doing business by exhibiting what he called a 'patent fish-tail' in a trough of water.

"He used to wear a semi-military uniform, with spurs, and carried a lady's riding whip in his hand . . . He posed at various times, as a litterateur, a journalist, a diplomatist, a Government agent, an officer of the British army in

Actual handwriting of Major Byron.

the East Indies, a British naval officer, an officer of the United States Army, a mining prospector, a broker, a merchant, a spy, an agent for cotton claims, a commission agent, an Oriental traveler, a representative of European mercantile interests, a bookseller, a patent rights agent, a gentleman of means, and an aristocratic exile, expatriated and pensioned on condition that he should never reveal his genealogy."

Far more interesting than his own disreputable career was the romantic life story he spun for himself. In his mythical identity, his mother was the Countess De Luna, a beautiful Jew (or Catholic), of the purest Spanish blood with whom the great Lord Byron became enamoured on his first visit to Spain. The handsome poet married her in rites of the Catholic church [this does not sound like Byron!] and on his return to England had the marriage disavowed as illegal so that he could carry on without guilt his romantic escapades. The countess gave birth to a son—George Gordon De Luna Byron.

The major fancied himself a Childe Harold, and in one letter described his pilgrimage "over the Orient; from the City of the Sultan to the Cataracts of the Nile; from Mount Ararat to the Mouth of the Ganges." He visited Byron's grave and in Spain shed tears over the grave of his "mother."

"If I omit an apology for addressing you," he wrote in an amazing "autobiographical" letter to John Murray, "let me hope that a son of the late Lord Byron, whose esteem and friendship you possessed in so eminent a degree, may without apprehension appeal to your kindness, and succeed perhaps in conciliating your good graces.

"You will, no doubt, be startled by these news—but of the birth of a son to Lord Byron he, himself, remained ignorant till a short time before his premature death in Greece, and to the world at large family considerations have always kept this fact secret. If I disclose it now to a friend of the late Lord B., it is because my embarrassing circumstances compel me to do so . . ."

Major Byron continues his story with a vague account of his education in Paris: "My heart full of strong and ardent passions, my imagination vivid and uncontrolled, with some knowledge gained from books, and some shrewd sense of my own, but with little self-government, and no experience, I set out from Paris to return to Spain. The buoyancy of my youth, the spring vigor of my muscles, and a good deal of imagination, gave me a sort of indescribable passion for adventure from my childhood, which required even the stimulus of danger to satisfy;—and it needed many a hard morsel from the rough hand of the world to quell such a spirit's appetite for excitement.

"My only resource at present is like the ostrich in the fable, to shut my eyes against the evils that pursue me, filling up the vacuity of each moment with any circumstances less painful than my own thoughts, and leaving to time—the great patron of the unfortunate—to remove my difficulties, and provide for my wants. Do not, Sir, suppose me to be faint hearted—I am a Byron,—the bar sinister notwithstanding—Civil law cannot change nature."

When this and similar hat-in-hand approaches met with no response, Major Byron launched himself in the amazing career that was to upend the whole world of literary scholarship. He announced that he planned to write a biography of Lord Byron, and he appealed for letters of the famed poet. Hundreds poured in. The major did write several installments of the biography, giving personal reminiscences or opinions of Lord Byron's work and life, but he quickly abandoned this first really noble effort for the speedier profits of selling the autograph letters which had been sent to him, in most cases, merely to be copied. When the supply of original letters ran out, the self-announced bastard Byron began forging another supply. Then he added Shelley and Keats to his fabricated wares. In 1872, the forged Byron letters showed up in London. Some were bought by Byron's own publisher who was utterly taken in by the adroit imitation of the style and script of the great poet.

Nineteen of Major Byron's forgeries were published in a rare volume, *The Unpublished Letters of Lord Byron* (1872), and half a century later were proclaimed genuine by the eminent critic (and forger!), Thomas J. Wise. And I must reluctantly admit that, when in college, I read these nineteen forged missives to "Dearest L" and was absolutely fetched by them. I even set out to prove, as Murray and Wise had believed, that they were genuine. But in the space of a single afternoon I had piled up enough damning evidence to establish beyond all doubt their spurious nature. I now own a special printing of them in a slender, beautiful little volume which is a delight to read. Sometimes of a winter night I crowd myself up under the bed covers and peruse these letters. I like to pretend they are not forgeries, because I consider them literature in their own right. For, unless one probes hard into the dates and names and places, the forgeries of Major Byron would trap even the most cautious Byronite.

Oh, the clever scoundrel! When he waxes Byronic one envisions again the handsome, haughty profile, the limp, the flung-back cape. There are in his forgeries all the urbanity and arrogance and cynicism which one encounters in the letters of the great poet himself:

"I am not all black—indeed rather pie-bald . . ."

"I . . . am damned and dunned to death by Christians and creditors, though, God knows, I am bad and poor

such a token of remembrance. — I must not forget- M^rs* Hanson who has often been a mother to me, and as you have always been a friend I beg you to believe me with all sincerity yours Byron*

Portion of an authentic letter of Lord Byron.

enough . . . The child is dead: I do not regret it, though a bastard Byron is better than no Byron."

"I am married at last, and mean no disrespect to Lady Byron, who, though she may be a seraph to her friends, and really is, I believe, a good woman, is a devil to me. We have nothing in common, except disquiet; and Heaven knows how much ennui."

"I am misunderstood, flattered by women, pestered, cursed, hated, reproached, and forgotten to such a degree, that I am most grateful for the night and hail the morning with disappointment."

Could Lord Byron himself have put it better?

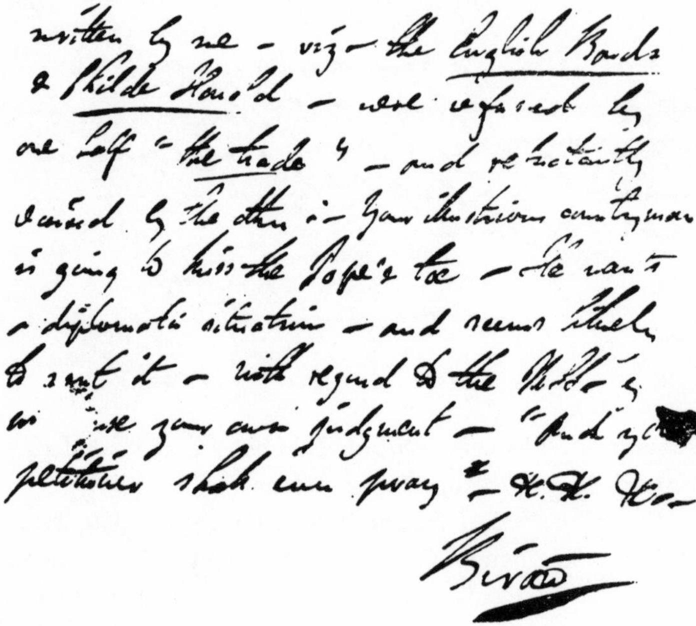
written by me — viz — the English Bards
& Childe Harold — were refused by
one half "the trade" — and reluctantly
received by the other — Your illustrious countryman
is going to kiss the Pope's toe — He wants
a diplomatic situation — and seems likely
to get it — with regard to the [illegible]
[illegible] use your own judgment — "and yr
petitioner shall ever pray" — &c. &c. &c.
Byron

Portion of a letter of Lord Byron forged by Major Byron.

Many years ago, when I first started in the autograph business, an old man came into my office and placed a battered folder in front of me, labelled *Lord Byron*.

"How much do you want for it?" I asked, looking over a three-page letter of the inspired lord.

"You name the price."

I told the vendor to come back in an hour. Then I began to study the letter. At first I was convinced that it was absolutely genuine. The writing, the address-leaf with contemporary stamped postmarks—all were unmistakably Byronic. Yet I was worried because the seller had so casually left the price up to me. Could he know something about the letter which I did not? Suddenly I noticed several stains near the bottom of the letter, stains characteristic of nearly all of Major Byron's forgeries. In addition, although the letter bore an early date, it was in the nearly illegible scrawl characteristic of Lord Byron's maturity—another mark of the major's work, for he employed the same hand for early and late letters of the poet.

When the vendor came back, I was ready for him.

"I'll give you ten dollars for your Byron letter."

Apparently aware that he was selling me a forgery, he accepted my offer cheerfully; and I still retain this choice example of the major's vagaries in my personal collection of fakes.

Thank God for Major Byron! He brought excitement and thrills into the moribund world of scholarship. His rogueries still bedevil collectors. His frauds and fakes are with us everywhere, even in academic tomes. His superb imitations of the author of *Don Juan* still challenge the most astute researchers.

Blow the dust off a letter of the great poet and what have you got?—a romantic letter of Lord Byron?—or a forgery by Major Byron?

7

THE PURLOINED LETTER
OF EDGAR ALLAN POE

There was no mistaking the beautiful cursive script of Edgar Allan Poe. Every letter in every word was formed with elegance and grace. My face warmed with excitement as I examined the superb letter which had just reached me in the mail, for it brought light to this dark, rainy day of October 7, 1965—the 116th anniversary of Poe's death in the charity ward of a Baltimore hospital. The letter had come to me unsolicited, an offering for my "next auction" from a stamp dealer in Baltimore.

Of all American literary autographs, Poe's is by far the most valuable and desirable. Many autographs are rarer —those of Emily Dickinson and Herman Melville, for example—but they do not command the same enormous prices or send the same shiver up the spine as a Poe letter.

For more than a quarter of a century, I had hoped to own, if only temporarily, an exciting letter of the great melancholy poet, master of the short tale, dreamer par excellence, and originator of the detective story. But so elusive is his autograph that in my entire career I have handled only a few trifling fragments and short notes, never a really fine letter like the glorious example which I now held in my hand.

While I am a sedentary man who rarely travels more than a few blocks from home, I once journeyed from New York to Manhasset in quest of an Edgar Allan Poe letter. My quarry turned out to be a forgery by Joseph Cosey, as is almost invariably the case. Long ago I concluded that there must be far more forgeries of Poe by Cosey than there are original Poe letters. Recently my heart made a short pause when a California collector handed me an envelope labelled, "Poe letters."

"Will you handle these for me at your next auction?"

I would, of course.

That is, until I took a glance at the letters. And a glance took them in as the too-familiar work of Joseph Cosey. The pale ink, the large, awkward imitative script, so unlike Poe's diminutive hand. Both betrayed to me the work I can identify at ten paces as Joseph Cosey's.

"Are you sure?" he asked, when I told him.

I was sure, to my regret.

But the letter that I fondled on this rainy October day was not one of the inept imitations of Cosey. It was unquestionably genuine. The first page had been trimmed away, but the two lengthy pages which remained carried eloquently the burden of Poe's song. He was soliciting from John Pendleton Kennedy, distinguished novelist and later secretary of the navy, contributions for a new magazine he hoped to start. It was a remarkable letter, written during Poe's years of struggle, and I guessed that it would fetch around four thousand dollars at auction.

"I believe I sent you, some time ago," wrote Poe, "a Prospectus of the 'Penn Magazine,' the scheme of which was broken up by the breaking up of the banks. The name will be preserved—and the general intentions, of that journal. A rigorous independence shall be my watchword still—truth, not so much for truth's sake, as for the sake of the novelty of the thing. But the chief feature will be that of contributions from the most distinguished pens (of America) exclusively; or if this plan cannot be wholly carried out, we propose at least to procure the aid of some five or six of the most distinguished —admitting few articles from other sources—none of which are not of a high order of merit. We shall endeavour to engage the permanent services of yourself, Mr. Irving, Mr. Cooper, Mr. Paulding, Mr. Longfellow, Mr. Bryant, Mr. Halleck, Mr. Willis, and, perhaps, one or two more. In fact, as before said; our success in making these engagements, is a condition, without which the Magazine will not go into operation; and my immediate object in addressing you now, is to ascertain how far we may look to yourself for aid . . ."

As I held this letter, carefully unfolding a tiny corner crease, I had what Poe might have termed "a gloomy and sinister foreboding." I knew, of course, that Poe's correspondence with J.P. Kennedy had been published but so have virtually all extant letters of the great poet. From the top shelf of my office library I took down my two-volume set of Poe's letters and proceeded to check the ownership of this letter against the footnote references.

A few seconds later I found the letter, with a footnote which proclaimed that it belonged to the Boston Peabody Institute.

When I read that footnote, I suddenly felt a great sense of personal loss.

"Get the Peabody Institute in Boston on the phone," I said to my secretary. "I think we have a piece of hot merchandise here."

My secretary telephoned the Boston Peabody Institute. They checked, and checked, and checked, and found no record of the letter.

My hopes rose modestly. Perhaps the correspondence with Kennedy had only been on loan to the Peabody. But, at the suggestion of the librarian, I tried the Peabody Institute Library in Baltimore.

Frank N. Jones, the director, checked his records and confirmed my fears. Yes, he said, the letter had been cut or torn out of a volume of manuscript Poe letters in the library.

"I'll get the letter back to you as quickly as possible," I told him.

I notified the Associated Press that I had received and was returning the letter; but, in response to their inquiries, Jones refused to confirm or deny that anything was missing from the library. Nor would he admit that the letter was part of the library's exhibits.

Charles Hamilton at work in his office.

Here was a mystery as bizarre as some of the best of Poe's fiction, including the celebrated, *The Purloined Letter*. By whom had the tight-security rare book and manuscript room been looted? What clever thief had made off with this precious letter—and how many other priceless autographs had he stolen?

The following morning Jones ended his silence, admitting that over the previous weekend, according to the library's register, the thief had been allowed into the rare book room four times.

Said a spokesman for the library: "We have nine Poe letters, all to J.P. Kennedy, and all bound together. The stolen fragment is part of the two-page letter in the collection and the thief, possibly interested only in the postal markings on the address-leaf, removed only the second page. The second page had on it an embossed library stamp identifying it as part of the Peabody collection, but the stamp was cut off by the thief."

Jones added: "I know of nothing else removed from the library, but as a result of this theft, we will redouble the caution with which access to the collection is granted. However, as in any scholarly library, there has to be a certain amount of trust in the library's users because it is impossible to check everything after someone has been permitted to use the library.

"I am dismayed," he continued, "about the publicity which the theft is receiving and I am afraid the thief will be frightened away." And he tacked onto this remark a bitter afterthought. "Mr. Hamilton is getting all the publicity while we're the goats."

But Mr. Jones' avowed concern about frightening the thief away was groundless. The next day a fourteen-year-old boy from the tiny Baltimore suburb of Towson heard a newscast about the theft and became so panicked and guilt-stricken that he went to his mother and confessed. She took her son to police headquarters.

His total haul, the boy confessed, was 139 documents, 15 from the Peabody, and 124 from the Maryland Historical Society. A Civil War buff, he had stolen mostly letters from one Civil War general to another.

All of the stolen letters were recovered, and the boy was remanded to the court for a psychiatric examination.

The case was now officially closed, but Jones' recrimination that I had got the publicity and he was the goat merits a comment.

As custodian of a great American library, filled with precious and irreplaceable rare books and manuscripts, Jones certainly has the authority and the privilege, if he wishes, to admit fourteen-year-old boys unchaperoned into a room containing millions of dollars worth of historic treasures.

But if, by accident, he admits a juvenile thief, is it sensible or proper to berate the person who discloses the theft and helps to recover the stolen property?

8

THE BOY FORGER

William Henry Ireland was seventeen years old—a scalawag with a long sharp nose and an inquisitive face softened by the dreamy eyes of an incurable romantic. From his famous antiquarian father, Samuel Ireland, William had early acquired a taste for the crackle of antique parchment and the creamy softness of old paper. Later, as apprentice to a barrister, he delighted in the opportunities to examine the court hand and chancery of ancient vellum deeds; and he relished the study of curious and long-outmoded scrawls. While other boys his age were collecting romantic conquests, this eighteenth century Miniver Cheevy was gathering ancient armor. Like his father, young William dwelt in a past filled with color and pageantry. At night, when the moonlight flooded his room, he envisioned his array of iron clothing filled with flesh-and-blood warriors. In his *Confessions* Ireland tells us:

"I have often sighed to become the inmate of some gloomy castle, that having lost my way upon a dreary

Drawn from the Life & Etch'd by Silvester Harding, 1798.

William Henry Ireland.

heath, I might have been conducted to some enchanted mansion . . ."

But Ireland's consuming mania was one he shared with his father. It had long been the elder Ireland's dearest ambition to discover an original autograph of Shakespeare. I can sympathize with this passion, for it is my own.

Even now only five original signatures of Shakespeare are known to exist—all in public archives—and of his manuscripts not so much as a dotted *i* survives.

Still, unable to resist the quest for the impossible, Samuel Ireland and his rascally son journeyed to the birthplace of Shakespeare, Stratford-on-Avon—partly to work on a book the elder Ireland was writing but partly in the remote hope of turning up some scrap of writing, no matter how insignificant, in the hand of the immortal poet.

But all they found were the same things that millions before and millions since have found—and doubtless many millions more will find: a cottage almost "flawlessly preserved" and full of "authentic relics" from Shakespeare's furniture and household equipment. The floors, which looked only barely traversed, were authenticated period pieces; the panes in the windows, while they admittedly looked modern, were guaranteed to be the very same ones through which Shakespeare gazed as his mind conjured up visions of ill-fated lovers and villainous kings. But the souvenirs in greatest abundance were those as familiar today as they were then—the boxes and other objects carved from the mulberry tree in Shakespeare's garden, "relics" which even then existed in such abundance that it would have required a forest of mulberry trees to supply the wood for all of them.

The Irelands had nearly given up hope of finding even an ink blot from the hand of their hero when their endless inquiries brought them to an enormous mansion where a man named Williams was rumored to have a great cache of old documents that had been in the house for more than two centuries. They were guided through the damp, cold rooms by Williams, a grasping old codger who was too miserly to pay the small tax levied by the Crown for each lighted chamber, and so kept all but two or three rooms in darkness.

When he learned what the Irelands were looking for, Williams said: "Why, it isn't a fortnight since I destroyed several basketsfull of letters and papers, in order to clear a small chamber for some partridges which I wish to bring up alive: and as to Shakespeare, why, there were many bundles with his name wrote upon them. Why, it was in this very fire-place I made a roaring bonfire of them."

Samuel Ireland clasped his hands and exclaimed, with admirable restraint, "My God! Sir, you are not aware of the loss which the world has sustained. Would to heaven I had arrived sooner!" My own reply to such a casual announcement of destruction would have been to seize the poker and cudgel this antediluvian moron until the partridges were orphaned.

So crushing was this disappointment to old Samuel Ireland that, on their return to London, his son felt he must find some way to soften the blow. He determined that since his father had never been able to discover a Shakespeare autograph, he would "find" one for him. William played the sedulous ape to the facsimiles of the only five signatures of Shakespeare known to exist. But perhaps we should let him tell the story in his own words:

"Having cut off a piece of parchment from the end of an old rentroll . . . I placed a deed before me of the period of James the First, and then proceeded to imitate the style of the penmanship as well as possible, forming a lease as between William Shakespeare and John Hemings with one Michael Fraser and Elizabeth the wife, whereto I affixed the signature of Shakespeare, keeping the transcript of his original autographs before me; while the superscription of Michael Fraser was executed with my left hand, in order the better to conceal it as being from the same pen.

"The contents of the lease being finished, and the signatures subscribed, I found much difficulty in annexing the seals, which, at the period of James the First, were not similar to those of the present day, being formed of malleable wax, and stamped upon narrow pieces of parchment hanging from the deed directly under the signatures . . . At length I adopted the expedient of heating a knife, with which I cut an old seal in two without its cracking; and having with a penknife carefully scooped a cavity on the opposite side to that bearing the impression,

I therein placed the strip of parchment pendent from the deed; and having heated some wax of less ancient date, I placed it when hot within the remaining part of the cavity, and thus formed a back to the seal . . .

"It was about eight o'clock, being after my evening's attendance at chambers, that I presented the deed in question . . . I drew it forth and presented it, saying— 'There, sir! what do you think of that?' "

The elder Ireland, of course, nearly collapsed from joy. Here at last was an authentic relic of the world's greatest poet! The next day he spread the good news. Scholars came to see the find and pronounced it authentic. Quite by accident young Ireland had adorned Shakespeare's signature with a seal depicting the quintin, a tilting device used in practice by knights, and antiquarians at once proclaimed this to be the original family crest of *Shake-spear*.

How did the young scamp explain his discovery? Very simply. He had met a man in a pub who shared Ireland's antiquarian obsession and who had invited the boy to help himself to a cache of old documents; but the man insisted upon remaining anonymous. The elder Ireland accepted this tale. So did most of the scholars who looked at his fabrication.

Emboldened by success, Ireland forged a "confession of faith" for Shakespeare. This also won wide acceptance in critical circles and Doctors Parr and Wharton, both noted scholars, went into virtual ecstasies over this fabrication in which they discerned every characteristic of Shakespeare's style.

Young Ireland now gave himself up to the great bard, and out of his wonderful imagination recreated, in that year of 1795, the world of Shakespeare as it had existed two centuries earlier. From his facile pen came letters of Queen Elizabeth, Lord Essex, Francis Bacon, William Shakespeare—even the original manuscript of *Lear*, with select fragments of *Hamlet*.

The British Museum displayed the rare treasures. The great James Boswell came to the Ireland home, and, fortified by a tumbler of brandy, knelt and kissed the manuscript of *Lear* and blubbered his gratitude for the privilege.

Wrote Ireland: "On the arrival of Mr. Boswell, the papers were as usual placed before him: when he commenced his examination of them; and being satisfied as to their antiquity, as far as the external appearance would attest, he proceeded to examine the style of the language from the fair transcripts made from the disguised handwriting. In this research Mr. Boswell continued for a considerable length of time, constantly speaking in favour of the internal as well as external proofs of the validity of the manuscripts. At length, finding himself rather thirsty, he requested a tumbler of warm brandy and water; which having nearly finished, he then redoubled his praises of the manuscripts; and at length, arising from his chair, he made use of the following expression: 'Well; I shall now die contented, since I have lived to witness the present day.' Mr. Boswell then, kneeling down before the volume containing a portion of the papers, continued, 'I now kiss the invaluable relics of our bard: and thanks to God that I have lived to see them!' Having kissed the volume with every token of reverence, Mr. Boswell shortly after quitted Mr. Ireland's house: and though I believe he revisited the papers on some future occasions, yet that was the only time I was honoured with a sight of Mr. James Boswell."

Later Ireland confessed: "Fired with the idea of possessing genius to which I never aspired, and full of the conviction that my style had so far imitated Shakespeare's . . . I paid little attention to the sober dictates of reason, and thus implicitly yielded myself to the snare which afterwards proved to me the source of indescribable pain and unhappiness."

Now, the history of forgeries abounds with tales of audacious rogues—bold, enterprising deceivers who would dare almost anything. One crafty fellow even forged the letter in which Columbus described the discovery of America, the very one which Columbus had thrown overboard in a cask during a storm that threatened to sink his homeward-bound Santa Maria. Still, for sheer, unabashed gall the palm must go to William Henry Ireland.

Perhaps Ireland had duped so many famous scholars that he finally came to believe his own story. Their testimonials were given with such confidence that Ireland may have begun to confuse his identity with that of

Shakespeare. But whether he was supremely naive or had merely lost touch with reality, the young rogue ultimately surrendered his overweaning ego to the irresistible temptation—he wrote a play for Shakespeare!

This was the most daring fake of all time—an original manuscript play of William Shakespeare. Ireland created the plot, developed the characters, and wrote every line of blank verse without aid. When it was completed, he titled it *Vortigern and Rowena*. And, what's more, he found a lot of people who were willing to believe it was penned by Shakespeare.

It was the find of the century. Covent Garden and Drury Lane vied for the honor of producing it. The manager of Drury Lane, Richardson, paid an unprecedented price for the drama—three hundred pounds down and half the receipts of the house for the first sixty nights of the performance, after expenses!

With John Philip Kemble playing the lead, as Vortigern, the play was presented under the management of Richard Brinsley Sheridan. Although the acting was excellent, the poetry was bad and the plot even worse. In the fifth act there was a line: "And when this solemn mockery is o'er . . ." which, according to a spectator, convulsed the house with laughter. "Never did the wittiest comedy nor the broadest farce produce such long-continued and tumultuous laughter, and such protracted harrahing. The audience cried for an encore, and Kemble repeated the line, again bringing screams of delight."

After the play's one-night stand, Sheridan exclaimed

William Henry Ireland fabricates a few of his specialties. At the bottom appears Ireland's "confession," dated December 14, 1844, attested by both William Shakespeare and William Henry Ireland.

of Ireland: "Damn the fellow. I believe his face is a forgery! He is the most specious man I ever saw."

But the failure of his drama did not mark the end of the deceptions of Ireland. True, his forgeries were no longer accepted by scholars as authentic relics. But since the notorious fakes quickly became collectors' items, there were not nearly enough *Lears* and *Hamlets* to supply the market and Ireland quickly set about to meet the demand by forging his own forgeries!

Today it is quite a trick to spot an original forgery from a forged forgery. I have in my personal collection of fakes a letter of the Elizabethan actor, Nat Field, scrawled in the pale ink used by Ireland, with his quaint and very inaccurate Elizabethan spelling. But I have never been able to determine whether it is an original forgery or a later counterfeit.

The ultimate irony—in 1841 the last original Shakespeare signature ever to appear for sale changed hands at £145 ($725), while in 1964 a small packet of Shakespeare forgeries by Ireland was sold for £340 ($925)!

9

NESSIP SEVEN AND THE OSCAR WILDE LETTER

"There's a strange, furtive-looking man in the front room," whispered my secretary, June Keller, placing a letter of Oscar Wilde on my desk. "He says he owns this letter and wants to sell it, but he can't even pronounce Wilde's name."

As I turned the pages of the faded old letter, indited in Wilde's fastidiously beautiful script, I was so enthralled by its contents that I forget all about the "furtive-looking man" who was waiting for my decision. There is something about the delicate Greek-like chirography of Wilde that gives added piquancy to his penned words, and I found myself quite swept away.

The letter was devoted to stage-directions for the first production of *Lady Windermere's Fan,* and I was deeply immersed in the production of the drama by the time I turned the last page.

I felt I had to have this letter. In fact, so eager was I to buy it that I ignored my secretary's veiled warning. I would have endured the smell of brimstone to purchase the letter from the devil himself. I offered the stranger $350, at that time a huge price for a Wilde letter, and he accepted at once. As I signed the check made out to *Nessip Seven,* I was amused by his unusual name. Seven was never a lucky number for me, but had I then any inkling of the circumstances under which I would soon come violently face to face, almost fist to fist, with Nessip Seven, I wouldn't have been so amused.

No sooner had I bought the letter than I began to read it again, slowly, relishing every apt phrase of Mrs. Wilde's bad boy. Suddenly I was struck by the conviction that I remembered this letter from many years before. This was not a copy, certainly, of that original letter. And my recall of the physical appearance of old documents is so accurate that I seldom forget the looks of any letter which I buy or sell. Still, I was sure I had never held this letter in my hands, despite the fact that I somehow knew the length and contents of it.

Then I recollected. I had read a description of it in an old catalogue. I went to my library and within minutes I discovered that the letter was printed, in part, in the first catalogue ever issued by my friend, the collector-dealer, Rudolf Kallir.

Was it stolen, I wanted to know.

"Not stolen," explained Rudolf over the telephone. "I sent the Wilde letter on approval to another dealer. He decided not to buy it, and returned it by registered mail, fully insured. It never reached me. Apparently it was lost, or delivered to the wrong person. When the postal authorities failed to find it, the insurance company paid the claim."

Rudolf did not ask for the letter, since he had already been compensated for its loss, but he promised to inquire into the legal ownership.

After I hung up, I asked my secretary for the address given her by Nessip Seven. He lived in the same Riverside Drive apartment building as Kallir! A quick phone call confirmed that Kallir did not know him and had never heard of him.

I called the bank and stopped payment on my check.

Then I phoned my friend, Inspector George Forster of the postoffice department. I explained what had happened.

"You are caught in the middle of a strange situation," he said. "The letter may or may not have been stolen. More likely it was just delivered to the wrong address. But, in any event, it doesn't belong to Kallir. It probably belongs to the United States government, but I'm not sure. Let me check on it."

"What shall I do if Nessip Seven walks in and claims the letter?"

"Don't give it to him. Stall him, and call me. I'll get over to your shop right away."

Two days later, as I sat in my office reading mail, the shop erupted with violent sounds. The air was filled with recriminatory cries, some of them in broken English. Then June burst into my office.

"Quick," she cried. "Call Inspector Forster. Nessip Seven is here and he's furious about your stopping payment on the check. He wants the Wilde letter back."

I called George. He was out of town on a case!

By now the dispute between my secretaries and the irate Seven had reached a point where I felt my intervention was necessary.

I glanced around my office for a weapon, but there was nothing available except an enormous Civil War sabre, the sort of weapon which might have been useful if I had decided to charge Nessip Seven on horseback. And still the dispute raged in the front office.

Hoping I could evict him without a weapon, I took off my coat, rolled up my sleeves, and transferred my heavy gold signet ring from my left hand to my right, where it might be useful rather than ornamental.

When I confronted Nessip Seven, he leapt toward me, pouring out a steady tirade of abuse. "Give me thot letter. You no cheat me," he cried angrily. His volatile and handsome features, fearful and dark with fury, took on the appearance of an angry deity. I expected him to whip out a knife at any moment, but instead he attacked me only with unreasoningly violent language. Finally I took a half-step closer to him, and said, "If you don't stop this screaming, I'll throw you out of the shop."

He stood for a moment, half-stunned, with his jaws drawn sharp together in a snarl. I felt my muscles tense up. It looked as if he were about to swing at me, so I prepared to duck and then swing back. I almost hoped he would swing, with three pretty secretaries sitting there waiting for me to be a hero.

But unexpectedly he turned around and bolted out of the shop.

"Where do you think he's gone?" asked one of my secretaries.

"Either to get a cop or a gun," I answered. "And let's hope it's a cop."

Ten minutes later Nessip Seven was back with a police officer, an acquaintance of mine who had worked the same beat for several years.

"What's the trouble?" he asked.

A cascade of excited words erupted from Nessip Seven, but the officer quieted him with a wave of his hand. I explained what was going on.

"I think the best thing to do," said the cop, "is to go to the 17th Precinct house and put the whole matter up to the lieutenant. Let's take along the Oscar Wilde letter."

A few minutes later, after a leisurely stroll during which the cop and I chatted and Nessip Seven tagged along behind, mumbling and grumbling, we confronted the desk sergeant.

The sergeant seemed unable to grasp the idea of a dispute over an old letter. When the lieutenant came in, a few minutes later, the sergeant explained that "these people are fightin' over who owns a letter of *Orson Welles!*"

The lieutenant, a well-educated and alert officer,

glanced at the letter and noted that it was written by Oscar Wilde.

"Well, what's it all about, Mr. Hamilton?" he asked me.

When I started to reply, Nessip Seven burst in again with another wild storm of explanation and invective.

"Quiet, you!" said the lieutenant. "You can give your side of the story in a minute."

I explained briefly to the lieutenant what had happened up until the moment we stood in front of him.

"Now," said the lieutenant, turning to Nessip Seven, "let's hear what you have to say."

Seven pointed a shaking, accusing finger in my direction. "This man, he try swindle me. When I no let him, he say he is cousin of President of United States, John F. Kennedy. He say, 'I have you put in prison.'"

"Is that true?" asked the lieutenant, looking at me. But seeing my total amazement at Seven's assertion, he replied to his own question. "Never mind answering."

Nessip Seven raved on. "This man say maybe he get President Kennedy to ruin my business, destroy my home, send me back where I come from."

The lieutenant looked thoughtfully at the letter of Wilde. "If you have no objection, Mr. Hamilton, I'll keep this letter here."

"Certainly, keep it," I told him. "I don't know who owns it; but, in any event, I have no claim at all on it."

The lieutenant waved me toward the door. "You may

go," he said. "Not you!" he cried, as Nessip Seven began moving out. "I'd like to have a little talk with you."

That was the last I ever saw of Nessip Seven. But the story of the man with my unlucky number for a surname does have a happy ending. Rudolf Kallir got back his letter of Wilde, and the postoffice got back its insurance.

As for Nessip Seven, I never heard what happened to him. But about six months later, my secretary, June, was having coffee alone at the counter of the Mayfair Restaurant on Fifth Avenue when a darkly handsome man sidled up to her and said in heavily accented English, "Haven't we met somewhere before?"

June instantly recognized him as Nessip Seven. "I don't think so," she answered, icily.

To me she said later, "Thank heavens he didn't realize where he had met me! He might have poured his bowl of soup on my head." Then she added in a stage voice of mock fear. "And after I spent two hours on my hair last night!"

A LINCOLN TRILOGY

He was a man of legends that clustered around him, the tender, the touching, the bizarre, the tragic.

Almost every signature he ever signed comes with a tale attached to it. Every letter he wrote has, the owner will tell you, a significance beyond that of the mere words. And even his most fragmentary notes, all of which are avidly treasured by collectors, seem to carry secret meanings.

Thus in a unique way the signature of Lincoln has its own immortal touch, its own legends.

10

THE LITTLE GIRL WHO BEARDED A LION

It began on October 15, 1860, in the little town of Westfield, New York, when Grace Bedell's father brought
back from the fair a wonderful gift for his eleven-year-
old daughter—not bonnie blue ribbons, but a photograph of the Presidential candidate, Abraham Lincoln.

Little Grace, a precocious child, studied carefully the
face she admired so much. It was gaunt and hard as
hickory, with dreamy eyes set deep under cavernous
brows. But the still-beardless face did not look to Grace
like that of the father of a country. So she sat down and
addressed a bold letter of advice to the lion of the Republican party, a letter that was literally to change the face
of history.

Hon. A.B. Lincoln
Dear Sir:

I am a little girl only eleven years old, but want you should
be President of the United States very much so I hope you wont
think me very bold to write to such a great man as you are. Have
you any little girls about as large as I am if so give them my love

and tell her to write to me if you cannot answer this letter. I have got 4 brother's and part of them will vote for you any way and if you will let your whiskers grow I will try and get the rest of them to vote for you. You would look a great deal better for your face is so thin. All the ladies like whiskers and they would tease their husband's to vote for you and then you would be President. My father is going to vote for you and if I was a man I would vote for you to but I will try and get every one to vote for you that I can . . . I must not write any more. Answer this letter right off. Good-bye.

GRACE BEDELL

Amused by Grace's letter, Lincoln replied in his own hand:

Private
Springfield, Ills. Oct. 19, 1860

Miss Grace Bedell
My dear little Miss,

Your very agreeable letter of the 15th is received.

I regret the necessity of saying I have no daughters. I have three sons—one seventeen, one nine, and one seven years of age. They, with their mother, constitute my whole family.

As to the whiskers, having never worn any, do you not think people would call it a piece of silly affection if I were to begin it now.

Your very sincere well-wisher
A. LINCOLN.

When the letter of Abraham Lincoln arrived in the little town of Westfield, there was frenzy in the local post office; and when Grace picked it up, she tore it open eagerly. Some Lincoln authorities claim the letter was stained with her tears of joy, but Grace said this was not true, and she later recounted by painting for us a beautiful picture from her memory: "A slight skiff of snow was falling, and it melted as it fell. Flakes of snow fell on it as a very excited little girl was trying to read a letter and run home as fast as she could at the same time."

Grace's "whiskers suggestion" must have convinced Lincoln, for just two months later his thin, angular face was distinguished by a beard. The tough frontiersman now had the benign and paternal look which gave him the nickname, "Father Abraham."

On his way to Washington, President-elect Lincoln gave orders to stop the train at Westfield, New York. He stepped onto the station platform and asked for Grace Bedell. When she came forward, Lincoln picked her up, kissed her, and said: "You see, Grace, I let these whiskers grow just for you. How do you like the improvement you advised me to make?"

When I was a boy in school, I first read this story of the famous letter of Lincoln to Grace Bedell; but it never occurred to me then that I would one day hold the precious original in my hands.

Early in 1966, I was reading the ads in the book section of *The New York Times*, and I was startled to see an advertisement proffering for sale this very letter. Expecting to be offered a facsimile, I wrote to the owners, the grandsons of Grace, who were asking a minimum of $20,000 for their great family heirloom. Eventually,

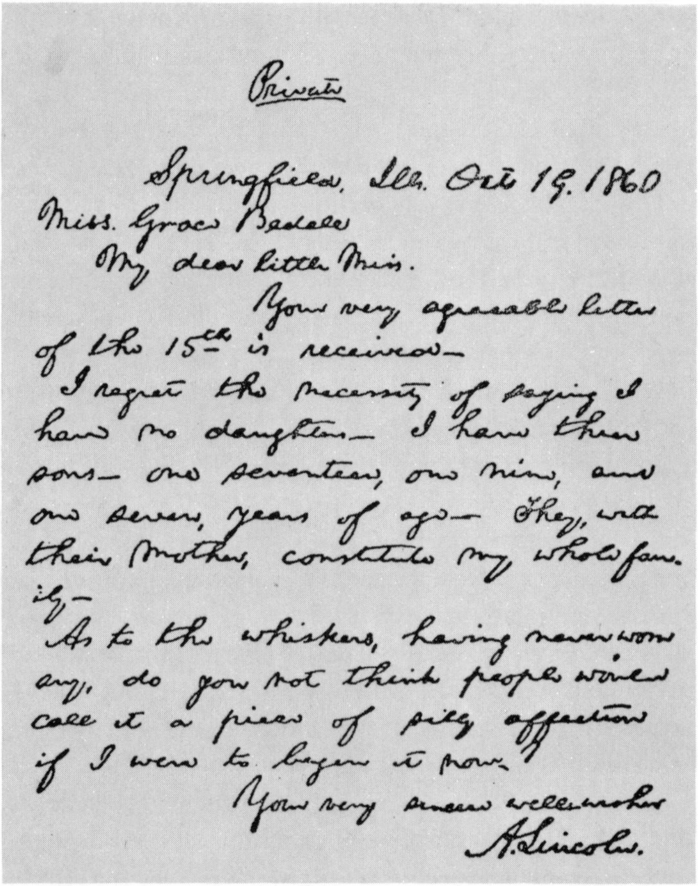

The famous letter of Abraham Lincoln to Grace Bedell.

after a lengthy correspondence, they agreed to consign the letter to my March 22, 1966, auction, with the agreement that if it failed to reach the reserve, their minimum price of $20,000, I was to receive no commission. I was to get ten percent of everything above that sum.

No Lincoln letter had ever sold for as much as $20,000 and I secretly doubted whether this letter, snow-stained and worn, could bring such an enormous price. But I was willing to put it up at auction just for the thrill of handling it. There were forebodings and warnings before the sale, and many collectors and dealers prognosticated that the letter would fall far short of the reserve and would have to be returned to the owners, the Billings brothers of Delphos, Kansas.

The day before the sale, I got out the letter and looked at it and turned it over in my hands, gently and affectionately. If it fetched $20,000, I thought, that would be more than $227.00 per word—as much for each word as the average short note of Lincoln was worth. Then there came into my mind the great romantic story behind the letter, and I decided that it was worth every cent of twenty thousand, that it would be a bargain at twenty thousand!

The next night the television news cameras filmed the knock-down of this now world-famous letter for $20,000 to the noted Hollywood producer, David Wolper, who later told me he was prepared to go more than double the reserve price.

Although I did not make a cent on the sale of this

Courtesy of the artist, Lloyd Ostendorf.

Grace Bedell
She invested three cents postage in
a letter to Abraham Lincoln.

David L. Wolper
He paid $20,000 for Lincoln's reply
to Grace Bedell's letter.

magnificent letter, one of the most fascinating and colorful in American history, it gave me more joy and satisfaction than any other sale in my career.

And, as a perfect postscript to the auction, the town of
Delphos, Kansas, where Grace Billings spent her adult
life as a pioneer, dedicated a monument to her on August
8, 1966.

11

"I'LL FORGE YOU A LINCOLN
FOR A DRINK"

First Joseph Cosey would show you his *A. Lincoln*. "One of my best creations," he would say proudly. "I fooled the Library of Congress with one just like this!"

If you praised his Lincoln forgery and offered him a drink, Cosey would get expansive.

"Take a look at this *Mary Baker Eddy*. Just watch how fast I write it. A couple of dealers fell for this one." And Cosey would make a few eloquent flourishes in the air with his pen before putting nib and Waterman's brown ink to paper.

Like a poet who swaps ballads for beer, Cosey, a little man with brown hair and a wen on his right cheek, would sit in a bar and whip out *B. Franklins* and *John Marshalls* with inspired facility as long as the drinks kept coming.

But this was in his palmy days, in the 1930's. Earlier, Cosey had been a commonplace thief, an ordinary crook almost ignored by the cops. Later he was to take narcotics and mainline his way into obscurity.

Cosey's real name was Martin Coneely, and he was born in Syracuse, New York, on February 18, 1887, the son of an Irish cabinetmaker. An unruly youth, Cosey was, however, a clever student, especially partial to American history. But he left school and home at seventeen to become a printer's devil at a salary of $3.50 a week. He moved restlessly from one job to another; and the hatred for authority, which he had manifested as a boy, was intensified by a four-year hitch in the army (1909-1913) which ended when he was dishonorably discharged for assaulting the company cook. Years later, after he had discovered his true vocation, he fixed that up by forging an honorable discharge for himself.

Before he turned to forgery, however, Cosey had a long career as a petty sneak thief. He was barely out of his army uniform before he replaced it with an even more confining one. In 1913, in Sacramento, California, he stole a motorcycle. He was caught and punished by a six-month prison term, under the alias of Joe Hallaway. Then he turned up in 1914 as Frank Thompson, trying to cash a forged check, for which he drew only a suspended sentence. But the following year he spent five days in a Seattle jail for carrying a concealed weapon. Again, in 1916, this time as John Martin, he was tucked away in San Quentin for cashing a forged check in San Jose, California. Three more sentences, all under his alias of Frank Thompson, and all for forgery, brought

Joseph Cosey.

his prison years to a total of nearly a decade before he finally developed, around 1930, the historic forgery racket that rendered him almost immune to punishment. Almost, but not quite. He was convicted only once for the forgeries which made him infamous. On February 24, 1937, he pleaded guilty to petty larceny and was sentenced to the workhouse on Rikers Island, where he served less than a year.

"I owe my real start in life to the Library of Congress," Cosey used to say. "I wandered in one day and asked for a file of historical manuscripts. I was intrigued, and when I left I took along with me as a souvenir a pay warrant dated 1786 signed by Benjamin Franklin when he was president of Pennsylvania. Later, I offered it to a dealer on Fourth Avenue Book Row. He said it was a fake. I decided to teach him a lesson, and I went to work practising the handwriting of famous Americans. Less than a year later I had the satisfaction of selling this same dealer a Lincoln forgery for ten dollars. Despite my skill at faking Lincoln's handwriting, Franklin pay warrants were always one of my favorites."

True enough. In my personal collection of forgeries there are half-a-dozen Franklin pay warrants by Cosey, most of them with the corners tastefully rounded and with dockets written across the face of the document. I suspect that if Franklin had issued all the pay warrants forged by Cosey he would have bankrupted the State of Pennsylvania.

Cosey's delight was to fool the professionals, but today

he would fare but ill. To an expert, his fakes are about as obvious as a purple cow and about as well executed as the same cow doing a *pas seul*. Cosey was always ecstatic when one of the biggest New York auction houses offered his wares for sale, under their usual "as is" terms. They still offer them occasionally, although I doubt if they have any idea what they are.

Most of his products Cosey sold for five or ten dollars, and by the 1930's he was known to many antiques and autograph dealers. His forgeries of John Marshall, Franklin, Poe, and especially Lincoln were familiar sights to those who handled autographs.

"My sister once worked for a doctor," Cosey would tell his prospective victim, "and when she left his employ he presented her with this." And then guilelessly, "If it has any value I'd like to sell it." Whereupon out would come from a faded envelope a brand-new forgery of Lincoln or Franklin or Poe.

Once Cosey defended himself: "I never impose upon innocence—only upon greed." But this was hardly true, for most of Cosey's victims were tradesmen or antiquers who knew very little or nothing about autographs and who hoped for only a modest profit from their purchases.

Cosey specialized in Lincoln letters and legal briefs. Sometimes he would take a genuine letter written to Lincoln (these used to be abundant on the autograph market at a dollar each) and add an interesting or unusual docket in the President's hand. He became so proficient at imitating Old Abe's scrawl that he even dashed

126

off legal briefs and disdained to sign them, letting the handwriting speak for itself. A supply of Monnier's 1851 pale blue paper helped him, for scholars often refer to Lincoln's legal period as his "blue" period because of the folio sheets he used at that time. At first Cosey used only

Three Cosey forgeries of Lincoln's signature (at top), with three authentic signatures of Lincoln. Notice that Cosey's forgeries are more legible and are written almost on the same alignment, whereas Lincoln's own signature rises in a series of three, and sometimes four, little plateaus, with the terminal *ln* almost one-sixth of an inch higher then the initial *A*.

Waterman's brown ink, with a few slight improvements, but later he devised an ink of rusted iron fillings which was more deceptive.

For all his skill, Cosey never quite got the hang of Lincoln's handwriting. If he had paused, even for a moment, to analyse Lincoln's signature, he would have noted that almost invariably the *A.* falls below the *Lincoln*, and that the *Lincoln* itself is formed in a series of two steps, with the *ln* on a higher level.

Cosey often claimed that his clients were as guilty of fraud as he, because they believed they were taking advantage of him. He claimed also that he was kind and generous. To illustrate his compassion, he told a story of a Poe letter. "I went around to this bookstore with a Poe forgery. The owner was out, but his secretary told me she was a student of Poe and would be thrilled to see something in his handwriting. I finally sold it to her for three dollars, but only because I was broke. Well, my conscience bothered me about it for weeks, and the first time I had three dollars I went back to the shop to tell her it was a counterfeit, and buy it back from her. But when I heard her talk about how much pleasure that letter had given her, I didn't have the heart to disillusion her. So I walked out and let her keep it and believe in it."

On another occasion, Cosey wryly defended his theft of the Franklin pay warrant from the Library of Congress. "After all, the library belongs to the people, and I'm one of the people."

Talking about Cosey to the Grolier Club in 1939, the late William G. Bergquist commented: "There is something intriguing in the idea of a person sitting down and deliberately forging the handwriting of some well-known person. Obviously this is not the work of any ordinary criminal. I am convinced that the person who does this is hardly ever motivated by the sole hope of monetary reward . . . Rarely do these forgers sell their goods to the unwary. No doubt, hunger or some other unsatisfied want forces them at times into the displeasing practice of selling a forgery to the ignorant, but certainly they get no pleasure in doing so and must feel that they are prostituting their art, for it is an art, rather than a profession."

But Cosey was far more than an artist. He had the audacity and *sang-froid* which characterize both the madman and the genius. His commonplace fakes—the Lincoln legal briefs, the pay warrants of Franklin, the letters of Mary Baker Eddy and John Marshall—all might conceivably have been fabricated by an ordinary artist-crook. But at least four times in his life the alcohol-inspired Cosey reached great heights. The first time was when he discovered an account book with the stamp, "Henry Anstice, stationer, cor. Cedar and Nassau Streets, opposite the Post Office, New York," a firm which Poe might well have patronized during his residence in New York. In this volume, Cosey created the genesis of Poe's "The Raven," copying out several stanzas, with manuscript corrections. On other pages, he wrote an accounting of sums due to Poe for literary work, including an indebtedness from N. P. Willis. This elaborate and convincing fabrication, a work of art in its own right, he sold to "Radio" Roberts, an old-time New York bookdealer, who consigned it to the Crown Art Galleries, on West Twenty-second Street, where it was sold with the estate of Max. D. Steuer, a swashbuckling art collector. In the maudlin assemblage of decadent art assembled by Steuer, most of which went for a fraction of what it cost him, the Poe seemed a great bargain. It was knocked down to J. J. Podell, a Wall Street lawyer, for $150. A moment later, a tardy bookdealer rushed into the auction room and offered Podell $1,150 for his purchase, but Podell felt it wiser to hang on to his "bargain."

During the next few weeks, Podell's conviction weakened to the extent that he consulted an expert and learned he had been "taken." The Crown Art Galleries refunded his money, and Roberts got his book back.

Roberts sold the book later for eighty-five dollars to a collector, who brought it to me for authentication. It was so perfect and exciting a forgery that I shelled out his investment for it, and placed it in my personal collection of fakes. Colonel Richard Gimbel, who owns the world's finest collection of Poe, including a complete transcript on oyster-white paper of "The Raven," heard about my Cosey treasure and asked to see it. I made the error of showing it to him.

"What do you want for it?" he asked.

"Nothing in my personal collection is for sale," I told him.

"But I *must* have it! I'm putting my Poe collection on display at Yale, and I'd like to set this forgery side by side with the genuine manuscript of 'The Raven.'"

"I'll be glad to lend it to you."

But Gimbel was not to be put off. "No; I've got to own it, because everything in the display belongs to me."

I had the feeling that Colonel Gimbel would have stayed and argued all evening if he had to, to change my mind. And I also knew that he would have been genuinely anguished if he hadn't got it. I yielded to the colonel's plea, finally, and let him buy this fascinating volume, one of the masterpieces of Cosey's art. Maybe Colonel Gimbel has more of a right to include it in his magnificent collection than I in mine. After all, I'm sure Cosey would be pleased to know one of his efforts found a place among the great Poe's authentic creations.

Equally exciting is one of the most prized items in my personal collection—a draft of the Declaration of Independence penned entirely in Jefferson's hand (by Cosey), with several important corrections. It is written on huge foolscap sheets of paper of the Revolutionary period and is docketed with a bold signature of Francis Hopkinson, a fellow-signer of the Declaration. So perfect is the imitation of Jefferson's hand that many of those to whom I have shown this false jewel are convinced that it is genuine. Is it not amazing that an alcoholic and dope-addict could attempt, and create with success, so superb a forgery?

Two other awe-inspiring products of Cosey's pen are an itinerary of the Lincoln-Douglas debates, written by Lincoln on a hand-drawn map, with the results of each debate briefly described by Lincoln. This great forgery belonged to my friend, Sam Moyerman, of Philadelphia, who recently died. I once offered him $75 for it. In my own collection is an amazing, authentic Civil War account book, to which (on blank pages in the original), Cosey has added some fascinating observations on behalf of an imaginary Lieutenant C.R. Rogers of the 109th Ohio Infantry. Most of Cosey's notations in this slender, leather-bound 1860 volume are modest inventions, but under the printed date, *Tuesday 20*, there begins a tale:

Last night Lieut. Kemp and myself captured a rebel who was spying on our position not one hundred yards from our position. He was a young man barely 20 years old and had apparently a good schooling and a good home, as he showed the ear marks of a good bringing up. He explained that he was a deserter from the Rebels and was coming north to join the Union army, and did not want to show himself in the day-time for fear of being shot down on sight.

As that was the usual story told by captured spies, in both armies, we told him he could join our regiment by obtaining a pardon from President Lincoln.

He was almost starving and we fed him of the little we had, and he greedily and gratefully drank the hot coffee.

This capture I knew would insure me the leave of absence I sought which in reality was to secretly hurry home and see if all was well—which I can do in two days—and return again—contented. I had not the faintest idea, however, what it would lead up to. But listen! I again made application for a leave of absence and my superior signed the application; and upon hearing of the rebel who was so bold, the commanding general approved my pass and I was granted 8 days leave of absence.

I went to Washington and saw Mr. Stanton who informed me that the President's pardon was necessary in the case of the rebel to prevent his execution. Execution by firing squad was the penalty on both sides for espionage.

Three days passed before I was able to see President Lincoln, and when he walked into the room where I was seated I was aware of a strange feeling of inferiority or something coming over me. I arose and saluted but the president waved his hand to the chair and said: "be seated, sir."

He listened carefully and very attentively to my story of the apparent education of the rebel, who was now under guard in our camp, and then told me it was a very serious thing for an enemy spy to venture within 100 yards of a Union position. He gave no credence at all to the "deserter" story, but pondered it over in his mind and then suddenly asked me if my leave of absence was to plead for the life of the deserter or was it to visit my people in violation of the 59th article of war! In all previous and subsequent battles I have never been in such a fix. If I told him the truth I would be branded, however secretly, by the President as selfish —actually taking advantage of a man about to be shot to further a selfish aim—and if I lied and said I came to plead for the life of the rebel, I forfeited all chances of seeing my people till the end of the war, however long it might last.

So I thought quickly, and knowing from hearsay what kind of man the president was I told him the truth, but I softened the boldness of it by saying that if the choice was given to me to go home and see my mother and family or go back to camp with a pardon for the rebel I would unhesitatingly choose the latter.

The president without a moment's hesitation asked me for a piece of paper—my pass, or any piece of paper, and I stood at attention and handed him this book. And in this book he wrote the rebels conditional pardon and granted my leave of absence, so that I was not charged with the time so far used.

Apparently Lieutenant Rogers used both the pass and the pardon, tearing them out of the book, but there still remains an autograph sentiment penned by Lincoln which is extremely interesting.

If my own collection of Cosey were genuine, it would be worth nearly $200,000. Someday I hope to write a book called "Cosey and Me," in which I shall recount my adventures with his forgeries. Often fakes are harder to buy than originals, and the motives of the vendors are as meretricious as Cosey's were when he produced them. Not long ago a woman came into my shop with a fistful of Lincolns—all products of Cosey's facile pen—and although she finally conceded to my proof that they weren't genuine, she nevertheless refused to sell them for ten dollars each as fakes. Sooner or later I'll see them again, I suspect, after they are palmed off on some unsuspecting antiques dealer. In the endless swirl of manu-

Lincoln forgery by Cosey in a Civil War soldier's diary.

scripts, documents and letters keep coming to the surface until finally they are incorporated into the collection of some great library or institution.

Many times I have identified a document as a Cosey forgery, only to have it offered to me again as an original within a few weeks by someone else. An amusing incident of this type occurred once when I was called to distant Brooklyn to make an offer for a letter of Poe about *The Cask of Amontillado*. As I entered a dingy, half-darkened room in an old house, where Poe himself might have lived, I could see in a far corner a framed letter which, even from twenty feet, appeared to be the handicraft of Cosey.

"Is that by any chance your letter of Poe?" I asked the hopeful owner.

It was, she proudly affirmed. I picked up the letter, worth about ten dollars as a curiosity, and pointed out the features which labelled it as a fabrication.

I'd have been spared a lot of trouble if I had bought the letter—but I said nothing further to the owner about it and confined myself to the purchase of a large collection of miscellaneous autographs which had been assembled by her late father.

Less than two weeks later, an antiques dealer burst excitedly into my office, with a package under his arm. "It's a letter of Poe," he said, tenderly untieing the cords which secured his treasure.

I shared his excitement, but within a few minutes I found myself examining again the Cosey forgery of Poe's letter about *The Cask of Amontillado*. I let the owner down as gently as possible, for his shabby clothes indicated that he was ill-prepared to accept a loss.

"It's worth ten dollars to me as a curiosity," I told him.

He shook his head.

"Okay, I'll make it twenty-five."

"I wish I could sell it to you," he explained, with tears glistening in his eyes, "but I simply can't. I put $200 in it—and that's a fortune for me. I've just got to pass along my loss to somebody else. I suppose that's dishonest, but, after all, you *could* be wrong, couldn't you?"

Looking at this wretched man inspired me to the ready admission that I was very fallible. He packed up the letter, still in the same oak frame, and walked out.

About a month later I got a phone call from a prominent antiques dealer.

"What's a good letter of Poe worth to you?" he asked. "And I mean a really *good* letter."

"About five thousand dollars," I said.

"Well, hang on to your hat. I've got one, and it's a beauty. Unpublished, too. It's about *The. . . .*"

"Don't tell me!" I interrupted. "It's about *The Cask of Amontillado*. It's penned in brown ink. And it's in an old oak frame."

"Why, yes. But how did you know?"

"Because I've already seen it—twice. It's a forgery by Joseph Cosey. My last cash offer for it was twenty-five dollars, and that offer still holds if you want to sell it."

There was a long silence, then a click as the receiver was hung up. I wonder who owns that letter now.

Cosey disappeared many years ago. Perhaps he died in a flop house or a charity home or collapsed on the street after a binge. But somehow, I have the feeling that one of these days a venerable grey-headed man of eighty or so, quite short, with a wen on his right cheek, will hobble into my office carrying a faded document and say, "My sister once worked for a doctor, and when she left his employ he presented her with this . . ."

And, for sentimental reasons, I will buy it.

12

THE BURIED LINCOLN LETTER

"When I was a youth in Illinois," the old man told my friend, a noted autograph dealer, "I met a most remarkable man. His face was brown and rough like leather and his huge hands were gnarled like oak knots. He was just about the tallest, thinnest man I ever saw."

"Lincoln?" asked my friend.

"The same," nodded the old man. "I had heard about him as a lawyer on the circuit, though he lost about as many cases as he won—maybe lost more than he won. But everybody liked him and some people even were predicting that he would be a senator some day.

"Well, I was staying overnight in this little inn, sort of a boardinghouse, in Pittsfield, Illinois. Late in the evening, Lincoln drove up in his horse and buggy and asked for a room. There wasn't one and when the landlord told him, old Abe's face fell.

" 'I guess I'll have to sleep in my buggy,' he said.

"I had a double bed in my room—a great four-poster with a canopy. I was sitting in the lobby while Lincoln was talking to the landlord, and I glanced up when his name was mentioned. Then I looked at him closely. He had one eyelid which hung lower than the other and gave him sort of a crafty look. Despite this, I liked him instantly, and when the landlord asked me if I would share my room with him, I readily agreed.

"Lincoln's frozen face broke into a beautiful smile and he thanked me with a nod.

"I wanted to stay up and chat with him, but I was very tired. I got into bed before Lincoln had taken care of his horse and fell fast asleep. Only once during the night did I wake up for a moment and hear Lincoln breathing next to me.

"The following morning when I got up, Lincoln was gone. I had met him briefly and never even exchanged a word with him. It wasn't until I started to dress that I found a note on the bureau.

"The old man took a paper from his pocket and read:

" 'Friend:

" 'Thank you for sharing your room with me. If ever I can do anything for you, be sure to ask.

" 'Truly yours,
" 'A. Lincoln'

"I thrust the message in my pocket and forgot about it. But a few months later, when Lincoln ran for the senate against Douglas, I remembered his note. There it was, still in my coat, and I took it out and put it away in my desk.

"Four years passed, and I had again long forgotten about the note from Lincoln. There were other and more pressing problems in my life. The Civil War was raging. My only son, who had lived for a while in the South, foolishly enlisted in the Confederate army. For months I heard nothing from him, and then came bad news. He had been seriously wounded and captured, and was under close confinement in a Union prison. His health was poor and might easily give way totally under the harsh regime of a prison camp.

"I was then that I recollected Lincoln's note. For six years it had lain in my desk. I took it out, and beneath Lincoln's message I wrote:

" 'Dear Mr. President,

" 'My son, Thomas, believed firmly in the Confederate cause. Despite my urging to the contrary, he enlisted in the rebel army. He was wounded and captured and now is very ill and under confinement in a New York prison camp. You promised me a favor once. The time has come for that favor. Will you let my son come home to me?'

"About two weeks later my boy showed up at our farm in Illinois. He had with him the note of Lincoln, under which was my letter, followed by another note which read:

" 'Let this boy be released at once in the custody of his father upon taking the oath of December 8, 1863.

" 'A. LINCOLN'

"I asked my son if he would give me the document, his actual pass to freedom, and he generously let me have it."

"Could I see it?" I asked the old man.

From his pocket, with infirm and shaking hand, he again pulled the precious paper. It was creased and worn.

"I always carry it with me," he said. "It is my most treasured possession. My son died many years ago and I have no one to whom to leave it. But I like to show it to everyone I meet."

My friend studied it carefully. It was the most fascinating Lincoln document he had ever seen.

"Would you care to sell it?" he asked.

"No, it is not for sale at any price."

My friend and the old man were silent for a few moments. Then my friend, fascinated by this unique bit of Lincolniana, ventured to ask, "Would you care to make it over to me in your will? I would be glad to pay you for it right now."

"No," said the old man slowly. "The document is already mentioned in my will. I don't care what happens to all my other possessions. I have never been selfish about anything in my life. But I have stipulated in my will that the document is to be buried with me. I want to keep it with me forever.

I said to my friend. "Do you know where the old man is buried?"

"No, thank God, I don't. He died about thirty years

ago, and I have often wondered where he lies. But I would be afraid to find out, for fear I might turn into a grave robber!"

The love for precious autographs is nothing new. When Alexander the Great conquered the Persians at the Battle of Arbela, he discovered in the tent of Darius a magnificent golden casket studded with jewels.

"To what use can so beautiful a casket be put, Alexander?" asked one of his generals.

"There is but one object in the world worthy of so costly a depository," replied the conqueror. And he placed in it his edition of Homer with Aristotle's manuscript notations.

During a wheat failure in Athens, Ptolemy III of Egypt (reigned 246-221 B.C.), noted bibliophile and autograph collector, received a messenger from the Athenians. "Our people are starving, O great king," said the messenger. "Whatever payment you require in gold or silver or jewels or slave girls we will dispatch to you at once, if only you will provide us with wheat."

"I will give you wheat," said Ptolemy, "if you will allow me to copy the texts of the original manuscripts of Aeschylus, Euripides and Sophocles. I promise to return the originals when my scribes have finished engrossing them for my royal library."

"But they are our greatest national treasures!" exclaimed the messenger.

"That is my price for the wheat you need," said Ptolemy.

United States Senate

WASHINGTON, D. C.

June 25, 1954

Mr. William J. MacPherson
56 Cornelia Court
Boston 20, Massachusetts

Dear Mr. MacPherson:

Thank you very much for your recent letter.

I certainly appreciate your writing me in regard to the three panel screen, but I am not in a position to do anything now. I am a collector of original letters written by outstanding figures in American history.

Again many thanks for writing me and with every good wish.

Sincerely yours,

John F. Kennedy

JFK:el

Letter of John F. Kennedy in which he mentions his favorite hobby—autograph collecting.

The Athenians sent the manuscripts and, wise monarch that he was, Ptolemy kept the originals for his private collection and returned the copies to the Athenians. However large a supply of wheat Ptolemy sent to the people of Athens, he certainly got a bargain, for had the precious manuscripts of Euripides, Aeschylus, and Sophocles survived the burning of the royal library at Alexandria, each one of them would today be valued at upwards of a million dollars!

Sovereigns and conquerors have always been partial to rare autographs. Napoleon himself had a passion for old letters and treasured a few in his private collection. Franklin D. Roosevelt was an inveterate autograph collector from youth, and I have seen many interesting letters from his pen in which he mentions his delight in gathering important documents of his favorite American heroes. President John F. Kennedy was an enthusiastic autograph collector and, in a letter which I recently acquired dated May 7, 1955, he asks a dealer to offer him "any old letters of historical interest." Twice I have handled autographs from the personal collection of Adolf Hitler, the more unusual of which was a magnificent letter of Frederick the Great, Hitler's military idol, beautifully bound and inscribed to the Fuehrer on his birthday by Rudolf Hess. In the letter, Frederick had penned a poem in praise of his own drunkenness! I have often wondered what Hitler, a notorious teetotaler, thought of this paeon in praise of inebriation.

143

FORGERS, FAKERS AND FRAUDS

Sometimes as I sit in my office I feel like a bull's-eye for criminals. I have been the target for dozens of con games and the unwitting recipient of hundreds of stolen autographs. Each time my door opens, I wonder what new offer confronts me. Perhaps it is something unusual: "one skull, in reasonably good condition, priced for quick sale."

Or perhaps the last will and testament of the beautiful Rebecca, heroine of Scott's Ivanhoe. *Or a batch of priceless letters of Thomas Jefferson, heisted only a few hours before from the great New York Public Library on Fifth Avenue . . .*

13

THE STOLEN JEFFERSON FILE

"Would you mind telling me where these letters came from?"

The young man to whom I spoke had a massive build and a fat face beneath an awful lot of thick, coarse black hair that needed combing and cutting. My secretary had introduced him as Martin R. Strich.

"They are the property of a gentleman who inherited them ten years ago. At the time he had little interest in them and he placed them in a safety deposit box. Recently he suffered financial reverses. He has asked me to dispose of them for him, and promised me a percentage of the selling price. I might add that these letters are only a very small part of the collection."

Strich was obviously well-educated. In the afternoon sun that poured through my window and gilded his features, he seemed almost like some ancient Aztec god.

The letters— "only a very small part of the collection" —were a magnificent file of missives from Thomas Jefferson to James Monroe—intimate glimpses into the mind and ideals of the author of the Declaration of Independence. And there was a letter from Benjamin Franklin to Noah Webster. I read it quickly, but it took only a glance to see that it was a unique fragment of Americana, for Franklin was writing to Webster about the urgent need for a spelling reform in our language.

"I beg your pardon, Mr. Hamilton." I suddenly heard Strich's voice. "Do you mind if I call my broker?"

I had been so deeply engrossed in my reading of the letters that I hadn't heard the question until Strich asked it for the second time.

"Go right ahead," I apologized, and went back to the letters.

But I couldn't help overhearing his conversation:

"No, I won't sell less than a block of 5,000." He pulled a pencil and a small black notebook from his pocket, and continued what was apparently a duel with his investment broker.

"No. It's 27-⅔ or nothing. 27-⅓ is the figure I turned down yesterday.

"Will you give me the closings on—let me see— American Tel and Tel, Anaconda, and say, how did my steel shares do today?

"Good! Remember, when they go to 44-½ I want to sell." Strich was sitting on the edge of my secretary's desk, jotting notations in his little black notebook. Obviously a heavy investor in the market! I was very impressed with his knowledge, and by the speed with which he made decisions and instructed his broker.

After he hung up, Strich turned almost abstractedly from his own financial manipulations and asked if I could make an offer for the letters. I suddenly felt that any sum I could offer his friend would seem to Strich like a trifling amount after his own huge stock transactions.

"The Jefferson letters are long and detailed," I told him, "and I'll need to study them before I can make an offer. But I'll buy the Franklin right now. I can give you one thousand dollars cash for it."

Strich didn't reply. Instead, he just stared at me, apparently bewildered. I couldn't tell if the figure struck him as absurdly low or absurdly high. It was in fact a high offer, for I had bought and sold many letters of Franklin for five hundred dollars or less. It was only because this letter seemed to me like a remarkable one that I was offering such a large sum.

When Strich finally found his voice, it was little more than a whisper. "I'll have to consult my principal. Is it okay if I use your phone again?"

It was, of course.

"Yes, yes," I heard him say a minute later. "I'm here in Mr. Hamilton's office right now. Yes, I guess so. Well, he tells me that he has to read the Jeffersons carefully before he can decide on their value. But he's made an offer of one thousand for the Franklin letter. Yes, that's cash. Oh, I see. Well, I don't know whether we could or not. I think it's a fair offer, but it's up to you. Yes. Okay, then, I'll tell him. Goodbye."

I held my breath as Strich turned to me: "He accepts

your offer for the Franklin, but he wants you to give me a certified check. He also says you may keep the Jefferson papers, but only overnight."

A certified check! I knew it was too late in the afternoon to get a certified check, and I just couldn't let Strich take that Franklin letter away!

I was frantically trying to think of a way to get the money for Strich when my assistant suggested we call the bank and ask them to verify that Strich could cash my check the first thing in the morning. He called the Chase Manhattan Bank and they told him they'd be glad to oblige. I breathed easier. I wanted the Franklin letter just as badly as Strich's friend wanted cash.

That night in my apartment I read the Jefferson letters over, and in detail. They were very important because of their political observations, and I was eager to buy them. But for some reason I felt vaguely uneasy about these letters. It wasn't that I questioned their authenticity— they were in Jefferson's hand, all right. I knew that scrawl as well as I know my own—better. And they were in pristine condition. In fact, they looked as if they had never left Monroe's study—just as if he had read them only a moment ago and placed them carefully in a dust-less drawer of a polished desk. Each letter was accompanied by its own folded cover, addressed and franked personally by Jefferson.

And yet I was suspicious. Maybe it was the still-fresh recollection of a theft from the Library of Congress of a bundle of Jefferson letters. I had spoken to FBI agents two or three times after the heist, and I was almost certain they had recovered those letters—and put the thief behind bars. Still, I couldn't get rid of the feeling that something was wrong. Could it be Strich himself? I was positive that he was honest. Why would any man with so much wealth at his command take part in a crooked enterprise? True; he was a little young to be handling such an important transaction, but he seemed very polished and easy.

"Maybe," I thought, "I should do a little reconnoitering before I go ahead with this thing." I asked my wife to check in the New York Public Library for any record of prior ownership.

At eleven o'clock the next morning, Strich walked into my office. No word had come from my wife about the letters and, laboring under the philosophic optimism that "no news is good news," I made an offer of $864 for the Jefferson letters. Strich accepted on behalf of his client. Then he pulled another letter from a briefcase.

"What would this be worth to you?" He held out a letter from John Jay to James Monroe, which even at a glance I could see was a clerical copy.

"About two dollars," I said, reaching for it.

But Strich suddenly jerked the letter back. "It has the owner's name on it," he explained, as he stuffed it into his coat pocket, "and I'm pledged to keep his identity secret."

"I really must be going," Strich went on, adding as he

151

walked out, "I'm leaving town for a few weeks, but I'll try to bring you more Franklin letters when I return."

Only a few minutes after Strich left, my banker called to verify the identity of a young man who wanted to cash two checks, totalling $1,864. I told him to go ahead and cash the checks, and Strich left the bank several minutes later with the money.

At noon I met my wife for lunch. She explained that she hadn't learned anything at the New York Public Library. They had never heard of the Jefferson letters.

"Why not phone the Library of Congress?" I finally suggested. "Maybe Dave Mearns could find out something for us." This was the call that finally gave us the information we needed.

"Are you sitting down?" It was the manuscript librarian, David C. Mearns, on the telephone. I sat down.

"Well, our records show that the letters you describe are the property of the New York Public Library."

I froze in my chair. I had invested nearly two thousand dollars in stolen letters.

A mere youth, Strich had hornswoggled me into buying a cache of Jefferson letters stolen from an institution less than a quarter of a mile from my office. Strich had so impressed me with his cool, deliberate manner and his knowledge of the stock market that I had abandoned my usual caution and become an easy mark for his hot merchandise.

The minute I put down the receiver I made another phone call—to the New York Public Library. I told them that they were the owners of the Jefferson letters, and very possibly the Franklin letter. It took the library about an hour to find and check the pencilled slips on which was recorded the only evidence of their ownership of these historic documents.

After I spoke with the library, I phoned my collection agent and good friend, Edward F. O'Rourke, and asked him if he could come to see me right away. Although something of an intellectual, O'Rourke is a formidable man and can be very tough when necessary.

This was my first experience with almost catching a thief in the act, and I was eager to return the stolen autographs to the library. It never occurred to me to call the police. I felt the library should do that, for I was sure that O'Rourke and I could get back the money I gave to Strich.

I told Eddie O'Rourke the story briefly and gave him Strich's address. I asked him if he would call on Strich personally, while I went to the library to return the letters.

"Hamilton, you fool!" he burst out. "You ought'a know that guy isn't going to give you his real name and address. I don't know how anyone so naïve can survive in a city like New York."

To all of which I agreed.

"Well, I'll get over to Park Avenue on the off chance that the address is legitimate. If Strich is there, maybe I can scare him into coming with me to the police, or at least into giving you back your money."

Of course Eddie was right. It was suddenly obvious to me. The chance that Strich had given his real name and address was very remote, and the chance of my recovering the money I had given him was even more remote.

I gladly left the matter in O'Rourke's hands, and I immediately set out for the bank, where I got photostatic copies of the two checks Strich had cashed, one for $1,000 and one for $864. Both were made out to him and bore his endorsements.

By 2:30 P.M. I was in the library with the photostats. The first person I met was Edward Morrison, the manuscript librarian. His lips quivered and his voice broke as he described how Strich had fooled him into turning over important files for examination.

"Relax," I told him. "You aren't responsible. Besides, I have the stolen letters here."

Morrison piloted me to an executive suite in the library where three or four officials were gathered, all of them with tense, drawn looks. I asked for the rare-book room register and they put it in front of me.

I compared the signature in the visitor's book with the endorsement on the two checks I had given Strich. The scrawls were identical. Strich had also put the same Park Avenue address in the register.

"Obviously not his real name and address," said one of the librarians.

By this time the news of the theft, the first in the history of the library, had drawn a crowd of nervous library officials into the room where we were examining the register. One important librarian, whose name I have charitably forgotten, said: "It seems to me, Mr. Hamilton, that you should have checked more carefully before making this purchase of stolen letters."

I bridled. Then I said. "You ask me to exercise care, yet the library itself fails to take the most elementary precautions. You put no identifying marks on letters worth a small fortune. Of course you rubber-stamp fore and aft a one-dollar book, but when it comes to a Franklin letter worth a thousand dollars you literally present it to the first amateur thief who walks in.

"What's more," I continued, "you librarians didn't even know that you owned these letters. You were asked about them earlier today and couldn't identify them as yours. When I made the discovery that they were stolen from you, you bumbled around for a full hour before you could find evidence of your ownership, and all this time the thief was making tracks. On top of that, you have no adequate record of ownership—nothing but a few pencilled notes on slips. It is lucky you are a public institution, because if you were a private organization and had to show a profit you couldn't stay in business a week with such slipshod management."

"It's all my fault," lamented Morrison, now on the verge of tears.

"No, it's mine," said an executive. "Strich came to me about ten days ago and said he was writing an article on the library. He asked me a lot of technical questions, like how many light bulbs we used every year, what our light bill was, the cost of painting and carpeting, whether or not the count on the turnstiles was accurate. He wrote everything down in a little black book."

"That little black book helped in my undoing," I sympathized.

"He convinced me that he was a serious researcher," continued the executive. "I gave him a pass that authorized him to go anywhere in the library, and he used that pass to steal these letters."

"Have you notified the police?" I asked.

They had, and at 3:30 P.M. a detective arrived. "We've had a theft," explained one of the librarians, "and we've just recovered the stolen material and we know who the thief is."

The detective's eyes swept the room and settled on me. "Is this your man?" he asked, groping for his handcuffs.

"No, no," exclaimed another official. "That is the autograph dealer, Mr. Hamilton. He has voluntarily returned the stolen letters to us. We have them here."

The detective listened to the rundown on the theft, and as he was listening, another library official arrived. It was John McKearnin, the security officer of the New York Public Library. While McKearnin and the detective were debating what course to follow, Eddie O'Rourke arrived with the news that Martin Strich actually did live on Park Avenue but was not at home. Incredibly, he had given his real name and address to the library and to me.

"We'll put a stake-out on his apartment," said the detective. "I'll take the first shift."

The detective posted himself in front of Strich's ritzy apartment on Park Avenue. At 6:00 o'clock he went off duty and McKearnin, working on his own time, took the detective's place, watching Strich's apartment from a parked car. By 8:00 o'clock Strich had not come back. McKearnin hadn't eaten supper, so Eddie and I took his place in the car.

From the doorman, Eddie learned that Strich had a rifle.

"He used it for target practice on the roof," said the doorman. "Took a few pot shots at cats and the neighbors complained. I'd watch my step if I were you, and not try to grab him unless you're armed."

Eddie and I decided to call in the cops if Strich came back. But we still hadn't spotted him when McKearnin returned. He had left his revolver at home, thinking he wouldn't need it. "I'll stay here all night if I have to," he vowed. "But I'll get the guy who robbed us." We told McKearnin that Strich had a gun, and then went to my apartment to talk over what had happened.

Hardly an hour after we left, I got a phone call from McKearnin, saying that he had seen Strich returning to the apartment and had called the cops. "Strich will be under arrest in a few minutes," he said. "Hurry over."

We grabbed a taxi and got to the apartment just as the police car was pulling out with Strich, and we followed in McKearnin's car to the precinct house.

At the police station, I was kept out of Strich's sight. He entered a small room with the arresting officers.

Another officer said to me, "We need your identification, Mr. Hamilton. Will you please tell me whether this is the young man who sold you the old letters?" He took me into a large adjoining chamber and slid back a panel to reveal a one-way mirror. I peeked into it and saw Strich on a bench, laughing and joking with two officers.

"That's the man!"

No mention was made to Strich about the theft from the library. He was held without charge pending the arrival of the detective handling the case who was off-duty and had to be summoned from his Long Island home.

I never saw a man more jovial than Strich as he smiled and chatted informally.

Presently the arresting officers joined Eddie and me, leaving Strich alone.

Suddenly, a few minutes later, at about 11:00 P.M., we heard gasping and outcries. Strich was acting as though he had swallowed a dybbuk. He writhed on the floor, foaming at the mouth and making weird noises.

"Epileptic fit," said one officer.

"He's faking it," protested another.

"We'd better not take any chances," said the first. "Let's get him to the hospital right away."

Half an hour later, while Strich continued to gasp and sob, an ambulance screamed up from Bellevue. Strich was loaded into it.

"We'll get him back here later," one of the cops assured me.

Eddie and I settled down to listen to the police short-

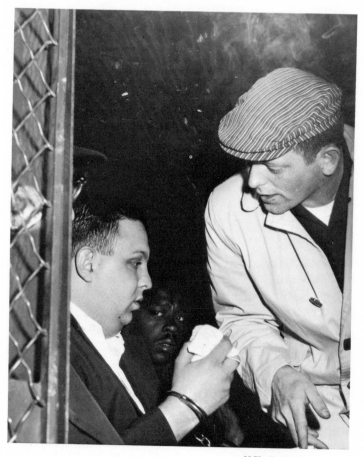

Martin R. Strich, handcuffed and seated in police van, talks to detective.

wave radio. Only three or four minutes passed before we heard a report of a head-on crash between an ambulance and a truck. All of us gathered quickly in front of a big wall map, and the police plotted the probable course of the vehicle carrying Strich. It was, they felt sure, the same ambulance. Strich might be badly hurt or even dead.

"Are you positive of your identification?" asked one of the officers. "Strich lives in a swanky Park Avenue apartment. If he dies while under detention we might be in serious trouble. At the least we'd be sued for false arrest."

I said I would identify him dead or alive.

The police were greatly relieved when we learned it was a different ambulance which had crashed. Strich, they learned, was safe in the hospital, under a sedative.

The time passed swiftly for Eddie and me as we watched the sad procession of law-breakers brought in for booking—a youthful burglar, a drunk, a prostitute.

The seamy panorama was interrupted by the arrival of the detective in charge of the case. He drove to the hospital and picked up Strich, now fully recovered from his real or imaginary attack.

Strich confessed at once.

The detective said: "Mr. Hamilton, since you have been so cooperative, I'm going to break the rules to let you talk to the prisoner."

The first words Strich said to me were, "I'm sorry, Mr. Hamilton. I needed money desperately."

To the detective, McKearnin, O'Rourke and myself he unfolded the story of one of the most incredible library thefts in history.

"Several weeks ago," Strich began, "I was in the library. I got to chatting with a man I never saw before and have never seen since. 'Do you know,' he told me, 'it would be easy to steal anything out of this library.'

"That remark set me to thinking. I needed money and I thought this was a good way to get it. I told the library authorities that I was a writer and was doing an article on the library. They opened all doors to me.

"The first autographs I stole—well, it took me several days to work up my nerve. Finally I asked for a file of letters and the attendant brought it to me. I suppose I should have concealed the autographs in my coat, but I was so unnerved that I scarcely knew what I was doing. I just stuffed them in a folder I was carrying. I was really terrified. I had never stolen anything before. When I left, the guard glanced into the folder and waved me on. The autographs I took that day I sold to another dealer.

"A few days later I went back. This time I took the Jefferson and Franklin letters."

"How did you know that Franklin's autograph was so valuable?" I asked him.

"I didn't. As a matter of fact, the attendant brought the Franklin file to me by mistake. Since I had the file, I thought I might as well take the letter out of it."

"Did you know that you left the address-leaf of the

Franklin letter in the file?" I said. "And did you know that the address-leaf had a library stamp on it?"

"No, I didn't know that. I wouldn't have taken the letter if I knew there was a library marking on it. I took only the unmarked letters. I guess I didn't see the markings on the other part of the Franklin letter because I was so nervous. I thought the address-leaf, as you call it, was some other document. It wasn't signed so I didn't take it."

"Would you have stolen any documents if they had been marked with a library stamp?" I asked.

"No, I wouldn't. I know better than that. The document I grabbed away from you had a library stamp on the back. I saw it just as I started to hand it to you and it gave me an awful fright."

"Where is that document now?" asked McKearnin.

"I crumpled it up and threw it in a trash disposal box as soon as I got out on the street. I was afraid to keep it for fear it would get me into trouble."

"Just one last question," I said. "Who was it you telephoned when you were in my office?"

"I wanted to impress you, so I called an imaginary broker. I phoned my own number, knowing there wasn't anybody at home. I was just talking to myself. I don't own any stocks and never owned any.

"The second call I made was just a stall. I was so flabbergasted by your high offer for the Franklin—a thousand dollars for a little piece of paper—that I needed time to think. I simply called my own number again and chatted with my imaginary principal."

"It's lucky for both of us," I said, "that you got caught now. You might have gone on stealing from the library and I would have gone on buying. You could never have made good to me on your thefts, but I would still have been morally obligated to return the documents to the library."

The detective asked, "Where's the money Mr. Hamilton paid you for the old letters?"

"I hid it in my closet. It's all there except for about fifty or sixty dollars I used to pay a few debts."

It was 3:00 o'clock in the morning by the time O'Rourke and I left the precinct house. I had an uneasy feeling that the case was not yet closed.

The library security officer, John McKearnin, whose alertness and determination led to Strich's capture, was reprimanded by the library officials for working on his own time and not leaving the matter to the police. Obviously they were hopeful that Strich would not be caught and disclose the ease with which he had rifled the old institution of some of its treasures. Crushed by the unexpected rebuke, McKearnin resigned several months later.

The rare-manuscript librarian, Edward Morrison, a gentle old man who was liked by all antiquarians, took the thefts very much to heart. A few weeks later he shot and killed himself with a revolver.

Strich returned my money, pleaded guilty, and received a suspended sentence.

14

HE GULLED THE YANKEES WITH
HIS BRITISH ACCENT

Moses Pollock, the Philadelphia rare-book dealer on
Commerce Street, was uncommonly sharp. He knew
books and history, and he knew autographs. And he
could drive a hard bargain. On this particular day—it
was early in the 1860's—his eyes sparkled with excitement as he examined a pass in the familiar handwriting
of Washington. True; it was worn and creased and
stained, but what a great find! For the pass was made out
to one of his own Revolutionary ancestors.

The owner was a refined, middle-aged Englishman
with an impeccable accent.

"Where did you get this?" Pollock hoped his face wore
the same bored expression that he had perfected after
years of bargaining with wary owners of rare books and
autographs.

"It was in an old hair-trunk. I found it myself," explained the visitor.

Pollock studied the faded document for a few moments, admiring the grace and beauty of Washington's script—a little shaky, perhaps, but it was hastily penned during the war when every moment was precious and there was no time for elegance.

"How much?" he asked.

"To you, Mr. Pollock, only fifteen dollars."

"Fifteen dollars!" Pollock was genuinely shocked. "Why, for fifteen dollars I can buy a full handwritten letter of Washington."

"I'm sorry, sir. That is my price." This time the visitor's accent was not only British but firm.

Pollock sighed and then counted out the money. But as soon as the Englishman left, he gloated over his treasure.

It was not until a few years later, when Pollock showed his prized ancestral pass to Ferdinand J. Dreer, a distinguished collector from Philadelphia, that he learned he had bought the document from Robert Spring, the notorious forger.

Dreer chided him in a tone of amiable disgust: "Mr. Pollock, you, of all men, should know better! This thing is an arrant forgery—it's worth less than nothing."

It might have consoled Moses Pollock, one of the great bookdealers of his time and the uncle of Dr. A.S.W. Rosenbach, if he could have known that this despised forgery by Spring would someday, as it is now, be worth twice what he paid for it, merely as a curiosity.

And it would doubtless have consoled him even more had he known, and perhaps he did, that dozens of Philadelphians from old and distinguished families gratefully invested ten or fifteen dollars in forged Washington passes made out to their Revolutionary ancestors.

Robert Spring was the first forger to personalize his fakes. Although he adventured now and then into fabrications of Jefferson and Franklin, he stuck mostly to Washington. Even today the field of Revolutionary War collecting is still booby-trapped with Spring's forgeries of the man who "could not tell a lie."

Very little is known of Spring's life before the law caught up with him. He was born in England in 1813, but as a young man he came to America where he opened a bookshop in Philadelphia. From here he carried out his transactions—legitimate and illegitimate. He bought and sold a few books from Washington's library, and the profit was so great that he decided to widen the profit margin on some of the slow-moving volumes in his stock. So he improved on them by simply adding Washington's signature to the title-page. To his delight, the expensive fabrications sold just as quickly as the genuine articles, and soon Spring was launched on a career of manufacturing Washingtons, almost to order. He did not, however, totally neglect the honest end of his business. To ministers in Pennsylvania and adjoining states he addressed the following communication, perhaps the first of its type ever sent out in America:

CIRCULAR

Washington

Respected Friend:

I am passing through the States, purchasing Old Books, Old Letters, Old Pamphlets, and Old Engravings. For any of such I especially want, I can afford to pay a HIGH PRICE. Many families have OLD LETTERS, BOOKS, PAPERS, &c. hid away in garrets and bye-places, of little account to them, but that would be deeply interesting to the Scholar and Historian, and contribute to throw a light on events of "other times" now shrouded in mist and uncertainty.

Should sufficient new matter be collected, a further history of this great country would be forthcoming; and it is judged correctly that much useful information may be obtained in this way. Do, therefore, allow me to look over any Old Books, Letters, &c. you would kindly, to further this patriotic undertaking, be willing to part with. I often pay a dollar for an old letter or pamphlet, looked upon by its possessor of no other worth than to kindle a fire.

Very Respectfully,
ROBERT SPRING

By the 1850's Spring was well established as a bookseller—and as a forger. Curiously, his own letters are of great rarity. Penned in a florid script, the few notes which survive discuss books or autographs, mostly his own fakes which he was trying to sell to unsuspecting customers. Once he presented a favorite client with a letter of Martin Luther, doubtless fabricated the evening before.

Unlike other forgers, Spring used two methods: tracing and freehand. When he could get authentic letters of celebrities, he traced them on a sheet of paper removed from the front or back of an old book, then stained his product with coffee grounds to make it look ancient. No

Signature of Robert Spring.

doubt this is the way he created his Martin Luther. But with Washington he was more adept. Spring had spent so many hours practicing the handwriting that he was familiar with every curve and flourish and could write Washington's script almost as swiftly as his own.

Spring's favorite was a Revolutionary pass. He usually offered this by mail, and the sales were most gratifying:

Permission is granted to Mr. Ryerson, with his negro man, Dick, to pass and repass the picket at Ramapo.

GO: WASHINGTON

So often did Spring forge this identical pass that one wag commented that Mr. Ryerson and Dick "might have constituted the first important traffic jam in American history." Another collector, who had invested his money in one of these mass-produced fakes and later discovered his error, suggested that a club be formed of all Ryerson-Dick pass owners to meet on the banks of the Ramapo and tell how they got stuck.

Almost as common as Spring's passes are his holograph checks of Washington, all drawn on the Office of Discount & Deposit, Baltimore, and dated between 1795 and 1799. How many thousands of these Spring turned out is hard to guess, but they are very plentiful today and turn up constantly at auctions where all lots are sold "as is." If Washington, even as a wealthy plantation owner, had actually written all the checks forged by Spring they would not only have overdrawn his account but bankrupted him. Like most Spring fakes, these checks may be identified by a shaky, rather diminutive handwriting and the reddish brown ink, quite unlike Washington's, used by Spring.

Finally, in 1859, the forgeries were traced to Spring and he was arrested. Spring employed both piety and wit by admitting his guilt and vowing to reform. But the moving finger moved on, this time to Canada, and under the female alias of Emma Harding. Emma, it appears, had a large collection of rare autograph letters, inherited from her husband and, being destitute, was willing to part with them. She was to be addressed in care of Dr.

Samuel Hawley, another of Spring's aliases. Quite a few replies, many containing money, were received by the bereaved and impoverished Emma, who obliged by furnishing letters forged to order.

Washington check forged by Robert Spring.

From Canada, Spring proceeded to Baltimore, where he operated under the name of Fannie Jackson, daughter of the late General "Stonewall" Jackson. Although Jackson actually had no daughter, the alias proved extremely successful. Spring got a list of British holders of Confederate bonds and, explaining that he was in dire need of money, offered Washington documents for sale. Pity the poor British, their portfolios already loaded with soon-to-be-worthless Confederate bonds, now stocking up on Spring's Washington passes and bank checks! Possibly Spring thought he could profit even more by a personal visit to his native land, so he journeyed to England. The British, however, were not gulled by his accent and he was quickly exposed and forced to come back to America where, under the aliases of William Emmerson, Thomas French, and Dr. Samuel R. Hampton, he continued to sell his Washington forgeries by mail, at prices from ten to fifteen dollars each.

But again, on November 4, 1869, he was arrested in Philadelphia by a Detective Franklin, the same officer who had apprehended him a decade earlier, and brought before the mayor. Sworn, Detective Franklin stated:

"A complaint was made here a few days ago, in reference to a man named Spring, who is a dealer in autographs, charged with defrauding certain parties, by passing upon them fradulent autograph letters. I went down to his house to see him, and found a number of manuscripts. He was earlier arrested in 1859, and came before Mayor Henry, charged with dealing in forged letters of General Washington. He then lived in Anita Street, near Tenth. I bought one of these letters myself. The paper he uses for these letters is prepared by himself, being generally stained with coffee. He frankly acknowledged his guilt yesterday when arrested. He also, earlier, wrote me a letter at my request."

"Will you please read the letter?" asked the mayor.

Detective Franklin read:

Philadelphia, Oct. 4, 1869

Sir:—Hearing there have been several complaints made I beg to state to you, from the remembrance of your fair and honorable treatment of my case with respect to the bogus Washington auto-

171

graphs, in the year 1859, that since I have resided in this city (June 6, 1868), I have never, by word or act, wronged any person in the United States, though I have obtained, in several instances, small sums from England, driven to such from dreadful home affliction, and to aid in supporting a large family of seven children, the youngest of whom died twelve months ago, at a moment when I had not a dollar.

I have tried by every effort to obtain a creditable livelihood, and it was only to spin out my short-comings that I solicited and obtained the small assistance I did from England about ten months since. I promised I would never do another dishonorable act, and with the exception of receiving replies to letters written to Europe before that period, and which, from my urgent affliction and often absolute want, I could not resist the temptation to keep, I have kept my promise. You know, Mr. Franklin, the affliction to which I allude. I am writing this under the greatest distress. I write this to you at four o'clock in the morning.

I am willing you should know all, and have it in your power to stop in future any dishonest attempt should I make any. In November, 1868, I wrote about eighty letters [offering forged autographs.] The replies were to be sent to Richmond, Va., and Baltimore. The Postmasters of Richmond and Baltimore were requested to redirect to Camden, N.J. I received, as far as I can remember, seventeen letters, three containing money. They were in the name of Dr. S.R. Hampton, and, of course, are all run out.

My second attempt was the [daughter of Stonewall] Jackson letters, which were immediately exposed in England, though not before I had received several letters, two containing money, £5 and £5. At the same time I wrote ten letters almost similar to the Jackson, from two of which I received £10.

Anyhow, I promise you, without any reservation, never again to use any dishonorable means to procure money. I will rather starve first.

Yours, in great affliction,
W. E(MMERSON).

When Detective Franklin finished reading the letter, one of Spring's victims, a druggist named Robert Coulson Davis, living at Sixteenth and Vine Streets, testified:

"I have known the prisoner personally for a good many years. I became acquainted with him through having a fancy for collecting autographs and things of that nature. He was residing in Lombard Street when I first knew him. What led me to know about these forgeries was that they were repeatedly handed to me by the parties to whom they were addressed, I being an expert in distinguishing such matters. I have also had several conversations with the prisoner in relation to the forgeries some years ago, but have not seen him since 1862 or 1863 when he left here and went to Baltimore."

Davis showed the mayor an album which contained a number of Spring fakes, including two of his old favorites, the Ryerson-Dick pass and a check drawn on the Office of Discount and Deposit, Baltimore. Spring admitted the forgeries, and at the conclusion of the testimony, the mayor set bail at $500, which Spring could not furnish. Ironically, the album of fake Washingtons which Davis had acquired from Spring would probably fetch today the very sum which Spring needed, for rogues always have an eager following, and adroit forgeries are avidly sought by present-day collectors.

Spring served his hitch in prison and when he got out kept his vow to reform. Without his skill as a forger to earn his living, he sank deeper into poverty and in 1876 died in the charity ward of a Philadelphia hospital.

15

THE RELUCTANT RABBI

Carl Williams, the Philadelphia antiques dealer, brushed a few cake crumbs out of his mustache with a tiny pocket comb, finished his tepid coffee with a loud gulp, and turned to me.

"Did I ever tell you the story about how I crashed Philadelphia society?"

Williams had regaled me with countless tales of his adventures, but he always had a large reserve of fascinating anecdotes. And I was forever delighted by his crude humor and Yankee drawl.

"I'd got a line," Williams continued, "on a real rarity that *might* be for sale—a magnificent Duncan Phyfe pie-crust table. Trouble is it belonged to an old dowager, a "mainliner," and I knew she wouldn't need the money, so I'd have to approach her with a different angle. I figured I'd have to give her a social pitch."

I had trouble picturing Williams in an elegant drawing room, balancing a cup and saucer on his knee, as he slouched before me now with his arachnidean legs

174

stretched far out in front of him. I sat opposite, curled up in a large chair, enthralled by the endless tales of my unusual entertainer.

"Well, I finally wangled an invitation to her house. She took me into the living room and we sat down on the sofa, right next to the pie-crust table. And I started pouring on the 'charm.'

"But the old gal misunderstood. All of a sudden I noticed she was moving closer to me. I slid away, kind of casually. She kept edging closer, and the next thing I knew she was cuddling up to me! Now I really started moving, but the more I sidled away, the more she snuggled, till finally I was desperate and I got up off the couch. She got up, too.

"Well, believe it or not, that visit wound up with her chasing me—chasing me, mind you!—around the living room.

"And all the time I was running I was trying to reason with her; but she wasn't hearing a thing. Finally she caught me, right in the middle of a big Persian rug. I tried to wrestle myself out of her grip, but she was pretty strong, and we both lost our balance and went crashing down—and guess what we landed on?"

I was almost afraid to ask. "The antique table?"

"How'd you guess it? Right in the middle of that *beautiful* pie-crust table." Williams seemed on the verge of tears as he recalled the ruined treasure.

"Was it broken?" I asked.

"It sure was! Two legs were splintered. I took one look

at it and saw it was hopelessly wrecked. I decided I had nothing to gain by sticking around, so I grabbed my hat and dashed for the door. And I never went back."

"Couldn't the table be repaired?" I asked.

Williams laughed. "Sure, Philadelphia style!"

"What's that?"

Williams explained. "When the big antique dealers in Philadelphia want to replace legs or other missing parts on valuable antique furniture, they make a new part, then bury it in warm manure for a month or two. It gives modern wood a real patina. Nobody but an expert can tell that it's not aged by time. A lot of dealers sell these 'cripples' as 'unrestored' and get huge prices for them."

There apparently wasn't anything about antiques that Williams didn't know. He was the author of the standard work on early New Jersey silver, *New Jersey Silversmiths*. At one time he had written a weekly column on genealogy for a New Jersey newspaper.

And, until shortly before I first met him in 1955, he had been in partnership with another antiques dealer in Philadelphia. Even at that first meeting, I was immediately impressed by his prodigious knowledge. When I asked him later what happened to his partner, I was amused by his candid explanation.

"Oh, we had a disagreement over the accounts. It was my fault. I'm afraid I wasn't cut out to be a bookkeeper."

I could certainly sympathize with that deficiency. Maybe our mutual weakness was one of the reasons I had grown so fond of Williams.

But if Williams had failings, he had at least one incredible talent. He was able to unearth some of the most fascinating and valuable documents I ever handled. He often whetted my appetite for a manuscript by telling me about it many times before I ever saw it—and I frequently wound up paying a fancy price. Williams was, among other things, a superb salesman!

After I'd been able to buy several beautiful items from Williams, I was approached at different times by two or three autograph dealers who warned me, in a vague and guarded way, to "be careful" in dealing with this man. But when I asked them to explain, they never came up with any specific complaint.

Since I'd had no trouble in any of my dealings with Williams, I felt that these innuendos were just the usual jealous gossip that abounds in the book and autograph trade. And I ignored them.

One afternoon in the fall of 1958 I was sitting in my office when Williams ambled in.

"I've lined up something in Philly I think you might like," he said. "Quite a colorful document, but it will cost you a couple of C's if I can lay my hands on it."

"What is it?"

"I may be able to get you the last will and testament of Rebecca Gratz. A fascinating document, believe me—not the will that was probated, but an earlier, unpublished one."

Rebecca Gratz! Her name is synonymous with romance. And I am partial to romance, as Williams knew.

The possibility of owning a will in the hand of the beautiful Rebecca, intimate friend of Washington Irving and the reputed original of Walter Scott's Rebecca in *Ivanhoe,* thrilled me. But I tried to keep my enthusiasm from showing.

"Get it," I told him. But I'm sure my face must have revealed my excitement very plainly to his practiced eye.

A week later Williams was back in New York, and he came to my apartment in high spirits.

"Good news," he gloated. "I have the Gratz document all lined up. It's practically your property. It belongs to an old rabbi, a relative of Simon Gratz, the noted merchant and autograph collector. Old Simon left it to the rabbi when he died—one of the few things in Simon's collection that wasn't willed to an institution."

My pulse began to knock again.

"The rabbi turned down my offer of $200," Williams said. "But when I raised the ante to $250, he told me that this was exactly the price he had in mind."

I reached for my checkbook. "Fine, I'll write you a check!"

But Williams interrupted me. "Not just yet. The rabbi wants to clear the sale with his family—especially with his younger brother. But it's just a formality. As soon as the brother says okay, you get the will."

Two weeks passed before Williams next came to see me. His face wore a dejected look and even his mustache seemed limp and discouraged. I guessed his tidings before I could ask him about the will.

"No dice," he told me. "The rabbi and his brother had a big hassle and the rabbi finally agreed not to sell. The old fellow needs money badly—you should see the hovel he lives in—but his brother is only interested in inheriting the Gratz will so he can sell it himself. In fact, he told me as much."

"Why not offer $300?" I suggested.

"That's what I did, and it really shook up the rabbi. He told me with that money he could buy himself a new suit and fix up his apartment. He says he's not going to live much longer and wants to enjoy himself a little before he dies."

"Suppose you offer $400," I persisted.

"Too much for that document," said Williams, "but if you'll give me a check I'll wave it in front of the old boy and see if he'll weaken."

It was three days before I saw Williams again. But this time he walked into my office with a slender portfolio under his arm and a look of triumph on his face.

"We got it!" he exclaimed. "It wasn't easy. But when I handed the rabbi your check and told him it was your final offer, he just wilted. 'I've got to get my brother's okay,' he said, 'but by Jehovah I'm going to get it!'

"He phoned his brother and told him he had decided to sell, and in less than ten minutes his brother burst into the apartment, storming and fuming. He was so mad that he grabbed the poor rabbi by the beard, and I had to pull him away. There were plenty of hot words yelled in Yiddish but finally the brother stormed out in a fierce temper and I came away with this . . ." and Williams handed me the last will and testament of Rebecca Gratz.

I paid Williams his commission—a handsome sum—and about a week later I reluctantly gave up my temporary ownership of this romantic conquest to a fervent Chicago collector. I had no inkling that very shortly the "romance" behind the Gratz document was to develop into a drama involving the police of three states and ending with my friend Williams behind bars in Eastern State Penitentiary.

A few weeks after the sale, a Philadelphia historian dropped in for a conference with me. He showed me a letter to a collector in which I had mentioned the Gratz testament. "Did you actually sell this will?" he asked.

"Of course."

"I am sorry to tell you, Mr. Hamilton, that it was stolen from the files of the Orphans' Court in the Philadelphia City Hall."

I'm afraid that I enthusiastically disliked my visitor. In fact, by and large I do not care for professional historians. They have a patronizing air about them, a ringing sarcasm in their voice, a condescension towards lesser mortals who they mistakenly believe have not committed so many dates to memory. Thus I decided to disillusion this historian at once, and said, with my iciest smile: "That's quite impossible. The will I handled had never been probated and therefore could not have passed through the Orphans' Court."

He replied with a smile equally as icy (and probably

equally merited by me): "Would you be so good as to examine this photostat and let me know whether it is a photostat of the document handled by you? It was made more than a year ago when the Gratz will, now missing, was in the files of the Orphans' Court."

I looked; and I gulped.

The photostat was an exact copy of the will I had bought from the reluctant old rabbi.

Under the circumstances, I agreed to get back the will from my Chicago customer and to return it to the Philadelphia archives.

Despite a few strong remarks dropped by the historian about Carl Williams' lack of integrity, I was sure that the rabbi and his brother had made Williams the victim of a con game. But, on the urging of my collection agent, Edward F. O'Rourke, I ran a confidential check on Williams.

I already knew that Williams had been in prison, because I had paid his attorney's fee and helped to get him out. About four or five months before he swung his big deal with the "rabbi's will," he had telephoned me early one morning.

"I'm in deep trouble," he said. "I'm under arrest."

"What for?"

"Remember that antiques partner of mine in Philadelphia?"

"Yes," I said.

"Well, he claims that I owe him money. He may be right, too. You know I never did keep accurate accounts.

Two detectives just picked me up and I'm down at the Mulberry Street station. They're taking me to Philadelphia. I've waived extradition proceedings."

I was so shocked by this awful news that I could scarcely speak. Williams went on: "Can you let me have a couple of hundred dollars?"

"Of course."

I sent a messenger to Williams with $500 in cash. Two weeks passed, and I waited in vain for some word about him. Finally, I called my attorney.

"I have a friend under arrest in Philadelphia—arrested unjustly—and I want to get him released right away." My attorney took down the meagre facts I could provide and promised to call back as soon as he could find out what was going on.

Late in the afternoon he phoned. "Williams is under arrest for fraudulent conversion—that is, he misappropriated the funds of his partner—and I've talked to his lawyer who thinks he can spring him if you can put up $750 by return mail—certified check."

I put the required sum in the mail at once, and three days later Williams showed up, tired and pale. "It was a horrible experience and I'd rather not talk about it," he told me. So I didn't press the matter.

But from the confidential report furnished by O'Rourke, I was stunned to learn that Williams had a record of two other arrests, one of which was for forging maker's marks on old silver.

As for the rabbi and his brother, they never existed.

Williams had merely been sharpening my appetite preparatory to stealing the Gratz will. When the price was right, he had simply walked out of the Philadelphia City Hall with the document in his portfolio.

As the author of a book on professional crime, I knew in theory the modus operandi for practically all con games ever pulled. But in practice, I had been hornswoggled by a simple variety of one of the most obvious—the old Spanish prisoner swindle. And no con man ever had an easier or more amiable mark than I!

Williams took it on the lam, and for the next few weeks I was constantly visited by detectives from New York, New Jersey, and especially Philadelphia. The object of their quest was Williams. They wanted any information I could give them about his habits, his friends, his hang-outs. I told them what I could.

One afternoon I caught Detective Walter Morgan, of the Philadelphia force, in a confidential mood, and he talked to me about Williams: "Williams is a slick one to grab," he told me. "I remember once when I was sent to pick him up. My partner and I knocked at the door of his third-floor apartment. His wife answered.

" 'I've got a warrant for the arrest of Carl "Moe" Williams,' I told her.

" 'Does that include a search warrant?'

" 'It does.'

"She opened the door and let us in, but I could see she was stalling so her husband could make a get-away. But there was only one entrance to the apartment, so my partner waited there while I searched. Finally, after having covered every square inch of the place and looking in every closet and under every bed, I decided to give up. On my way out, I passed the bathroom and took a final glance. Then I did a double-take. On the sill of the open window I saw, just barely visible, two sets of fingers. So I walked to the window.

" 'Williams,' I said. 'I can pound on your fingers just a bit and pick you up down in the court-yard with a broken leg. But I'm a nice guy; so I'm going to let you climb back in and give yourself up quietly.' "

"Did he get back in?" I asked.

"Yes, but we couldn't make that arrest stick. Every time we seem to have Williams dead to rights, he wriggles out. But not this time! I think we've got him now."

And Detective Morgan was right. A few months later, Williams was captured. "I'm glad you've got me," he said. "I was tired of looking over my shoulder."

On the evidence which I furnished the court, and on his own confession, Williams was convicted and sentenced in 1959 to be confined in the Eastern State Penitentiary for a term of two and one-half to five years.

That ended the story of the reluctant rabbi, but it started me thinking about an incident which began one afternoon almost a year before Williams went to prison. We were chatting in my office when Williams suddenly asked:

"What do you think I found in my closet this morning?"

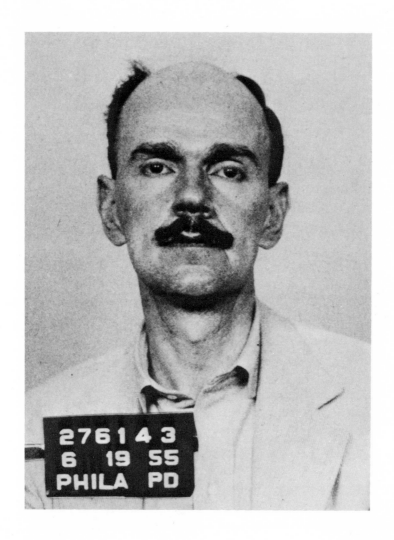

Carl "Moe" Williams.

"The family skeleton?"

He laughed. "No, but you're close. Just the skull. It turned up in a paper-bag. Nothing but a skull, and for a few moments I couldn't remember where it came from. Then it all came back to me." He paused, then said: "Did you know that they moved a big cemetery in Philadelphia out to the suburbs?"

"Sure," I told him. "When I was in the army I had a Philadelphia friend named Murphy who had worked with a cemetery crew digging up bodies in 1940 and '41. He was a football player, and he and his teammates, also on the project, used to run through their signals using a skull for a football. Sometimes they re-buried a skull on the wrong body. Nobody cared. Murphy told me there was an underground river running beneath the cemetery, and a lot of the coffins rotted. Once in a while he would open a coffin and find a watersnake coiled in the skull . . ."

"Well, I see you know all about the cemetery," Williams broke in. "At the time they were moving the bodies, I was a good friend of one of the descendants of the famous Peale family, and I was with him when he opened a letter giving him permission to remove, if he wished, the Peale remains from the family vault. But he wasn't sentimental and he just crumpled the letter up.

"I'm not very sentimental myself, but I grabbed the letter from him. 'Maybe we can ignore most of the family —they were merely great artists—but James Peale not only painted Washington from the flesh but was an officer of the Society of the Cincinnati!'

"At these words a glint came into the eye of my friend. 'Ah!' exclaimed he, 'I see what you're driving at. You think old Jim Peale may have been laid away wearing his gold badge of the Cincinnati Society. They're very valuable to collectors, aren't they?'"

"I assured him that they were *very* valuable.

" 'Let's dig,' he said, and off we went to the cemetery, armed with his crumpled letter. The sexton got out a big map, and discovered where the Peale family vault was, and we marched about a quarter of a mile with him until we got to some decaying obelisks. My friend and I pulled off a heavy marble lid, under which we opened a wooden door, partially mildewed and decayed.

"I had brought along a pocket flashlight," Williams went on, "and I shined it down into this dark pit. I could see almost nothing. Only dim outlines. And the smell was awful.

"Even though I was terrified, I put the light in my belt, grasped the top of the huge vault with both hands, and lowered myself into the darkness. I couldn't quite reach the floor of the vault, but I dropped down, landing on rotten boards. I got my flashlight out fast, and poked it around until I saw the coffin of James Peale, according to the markings made on a design of the interior of the vault.

"It was Peale's coffin, all right. It had been put on two sawhorses; but one of them had rotted, and the front of the coffin had collapsed and broken, so that the skull had almost rolled out. I was disappointed when I looked for the Society of the Cincinnati badge, because nothing was left of the body, other than the skull, but a dirty grey powder. Then I remember that in 1831 when Peale died there was a cholera epidemic raging in Philadelphia and Peale's body, like most others, was buried under a blanket of quick-lime. People thought the quick-lime would stop the epidemic.

"My friend yelled down to me, 'What's down there?'"

"Nothing," I answered, almost accurately.

" 'Well, bring up something,' he pleaded.

"I tossed the skull up to him, and then I climbed out of the vault.

"That was the end of a harrowing experience. My friend refused to go to any expense to re-bury the skull and presented it to me. I put it in a paper bag and, until this morning, I hadn't thought of it in years."

"If it's for sale," I said, "I think I know a possible buyer. It's Charles C. Sellers, the noted authority on the Peale family."

"How much can we get for it?" asked Williams.

"Oh, about five dollars. Just enough to drink a toast to the memory of a great American artist and patriot— James Peale."

Williams turned the skull over to me, and Sellers bought it for five dollars, a sum which almost precisely covered the postage and the cost of a drink for Williams and a drink for me. We touched glasses to honor the memory of Jim Peale.

In retrospect, when I think back upon Williams' career as a con artist, I wonder just a little about that skull.

Of course, it *was* the skull of old James Peale . . . and yet . . . what an ingenious way to dispose of the remains of a murder victim!

16

THE MANUSCRIPT PARIAHS

"Dear Sir," wrote the famous photographer, Yousuf Karsh, "I received your letter today at my home and I want to answer you immediately. I know exactly what you are going through . . . I experienced it while my beloved first wife, Solange, was dying. She derived a great deal of comfort from her faith, and in so doing, she made everyone around her stronger, too.

"In my youth, I experienced oppression and persecution at the hands of the Turks, and many in my family suffered greatly or were massacred. During these dark days of World War I, I lived a constant nightmare, from which there seemed to be no release. Only the faith which my mother instilled in me kept me going. It was a miracle to me when my faith seemed to be rewarded when I came to the New World.

"I am glad that your faith is strong, and please consider my hand clasped in yours in friendship.

"Please write to me again, if you so desire . . . what subjects did you teach in public school . . . did you enjoy the children? I am sure that . . . you gave them much that they will treasure . . .

"I am sending you, beside the portrait you requested, a copy of my book 'In Search of Greatness.' I hope it may ease the hours of pain, and allow you to know me better . . . I travel a great deal, but I shall answer your letters as soon as I return from my trips."

As you read this letter, you were probably impressed by two things. First, that Yousuf Karsh is an extraordinarily kind and generous and compassionate man. If so, you were right. Second, you no doubt gathered that the man to whom he was writing is on the verge of death. If so, you were wrong, unless his cancer is like the illness of Charles II, who apologized to his court for "taking an unconscionably long time a-dying." The recipient of Mr. Karsh's letter has offered no such apology.

Instead, he is one of a despised and outlawed clan in the manuscript world—the pariahs who make all sincere collectors blush. No device is too outrageous, no trick too despicable, if only they can obtain a hand-written letter from their quarry. Their plan of operation is simple and usually effective. They write to the illustrious, not politely requesting a signature and a sentiment, but claiming kinship, sending valueless gifts, or posing as historians in quest of information. No sooner does their victim send a reply than it is converted into cash, usually at the shop of the nearest manuscript dealer.

This particular collector's approach to the problem of extracting a valuable letter from a famous man seems to be a very successful one. For the past five or ten years he has been writing his victims that he is dying of cancer. He winds up each of his heart-rending missives with a poignant request for a signed photograph or perhaps a holograph quotation to sustain him during his final weeks, or days, or hours. Who but the most heartless or cynical (or once-burned) could resist such a small request from a dying man?

Several years ago the photographer, Edward Steichen, sent this pariah a signed photograph, and wrote: "I am sorry to hear of your grave illness and to recognize your splendid courage in facing the facts. If you can keep this up and develop it further you will be certainly enriching your life as well as the lives of those around you."

The Earl of Mountbatten, known to collectors for his persistent refusal to send his autograph, wrote to him in October, 1966: "Thank you for your letter of 4th October with the grievous news that your cancer is spreading.

"I admire the courageous way you are facing your fate and in view of this I am making the first exception I have ever made, namely I am sending you a signed photograph in spite of the fact that I have neither met you personally nor been associated with you in any way, beyond correspondence."

The aging Béla Schick, with enfeebled hands that could scarcely move a pen across a sheet, used more than he could spare of his failing strength to send him words of encouragement. When our executive vice president, H. Keith Thompson, Jr., and I discovered that the great doctor was being so unduly taxed, Mr. Thompson wrote to Béla Schick informing him of the imposition. Schick replied,

"It is very kind that you have let me know about [this imposter.] Considering the letters I received from him, it comes as a great shock.

"The first letter was from an individual who wrote that his grandson was dying from cancer and asked that I write a note explaining the Schick test. The 2nd letter asked for another note as the letter had been lost and his grandson was heart broken. This I did—After some time the younger man wrote that his grandfather had died—He was his only relative and wrote that he was a teacher who was dying from cancer—This I answered with my condolence.

"His last letter I am enclosing but this letter I did not answer and I have not heard from him since.

"It seems unbelievable that any one could do such a thing."

When letters from celebrities sell quickly and for prices that make it worth his trouble, this pariah proves himself a real letter-getter by following up with clinical reports on his condition. His "grandfather" often writes, giving bulletins on the dying man, describing how his grandson has clung to life (by a "string," as it were) thanks to the inspirational message of his correspondent. The replies to the grandfather are also promptly offered for sale.

In fact, this man's dying-of-cancer business has now increased to the point where the scores of letters of sympathy which pour into his autograph mill require printed price lists, issued regularly to a select group of collectors, librarians, and dealers. If his cancer can be kept under control, as it has been for the past five or ten years, he should die a wealthy man.

Almost as successful was Ludovic Picard, who lived in Paris in the 1850's. At first he begged money from celebrities, but he found this cup-in-hand approach hard going. Barely enough sous came his way to keep him in wine. Then he made the big discovery that even a peremptory letter of refusal from a great man like Victor Hugo was worth more to an autograph dealer on the Foubourg Saint-Germain than the pittance he might get by begging. He now hit upon the idea of writing to noted persons, explaining that he was tired of life and about to end it all unless he received a few inspirational words. He put his case plainly. He was a neglected artist—or author—or composer—and would stay his loaded pistol only for a day or two, until his correspondent could give him some cogent reason why he should cling to life.

The wary Charles Dickens, daily the target of clever, often crafty, autograph seekers, fell into the trap. He wrote to Picard in French, urging him to be brave and face his troubles with resignation. Heinrich Heine, lying on his "mattress grave," with both eyes shut by advanced syphillis, held up one eyelid with his left hand so he could write a glowing letter of encouragement. So did George Sand and Alexandre Dumas and dozens of others. And no sooner did Picard get their letters than he transformed them into franc notes which he at once invested in wine.

He was ultimately discovered by Jules Sandeau, the French author, who was so overcome with sympathy for Picard that he paid him a personal visit. He found Picard, not holding a pistol to his temple, but living it up with some friends in a cabaret. Sandeau exposed Picard in print, thus ending the imposture.

One of the most villainous of manuscript parasites was Ben W. Austin of Sioux City, Iowa, who in the 1880's worked out a clever plan for relieving celebrities of their autographs. He founded an imaginary association, *The Northwestern Literary and Historical Society,* with himself as secretary, and with a fictitious George D. Chester, D.D., L.L.D. as president. Equipped with seal and stationery, he proceeded, as secretary, to write to noted persons throughout the world, informing them that they had been elected to honorary membership in the society. Letters of gratitude for this "honor" came from distinguished men all over Europe and America. Austin was never satisfied, however, with merely a letter. In a follow-up, he asked for a manuscript for the "Society's" archives.

Fully as reprehensible are the activities of a philatelic association in one of our southern states, an organization designed not to promote philately but to extract autographs from noted persons. Before me lies a letter, signed by an official of that group, addressed to the distinguished poet, Karl Shapiro, which reads:

"Our Society would very much like to have your signature. Preferably on the famous poem of yours, 'Construction.' We would be delighted if you could right [sic] this for us in your own hand. Thank you for your time and effort. We appreciate it immensely."

Shapiro scrawled his name in red ink on the letter itself, and within a week or two it was sold on the autograph market. And I recall seeing a letter of Ira Gershwin who, although he acceded to their request for a holograph manuscript of "By Straus," noted wryly, "if you are what you say you are . . ."

One of the most successful of the manuscript pariahs who eluded detection throughout his life and even managed to get a Pulitzer prize was the noted editor, Edward W. Bok. As a lad of 14, I read Bok's *Autobiography* and was enthralled by it, and especially was I intrigued by his autograph collection, described in detail, and by his adventures while assembling it. Recently when I re-read the book, it struck me as the mealy-mouthed, pious, self-glorification of a pushy immigrant boy. But perhaps my opinion was influenced by the discovery that Bok did not always tell the truth.

About ten years ago, I ran across a letter of Alfred Tennyson addressed to "My dear young namesake." The contents of it seemed familiar, and I recalled reading a portion of this same letter in Bok's *Autobiography*. I checked, and found the passage: "Tennyson wrote out a stanza or two of 'The Brook,' upon condition that Edward would not again use the word 'awful,' which the poet said 'is slang for very,' and 'I hate slang.' "

An accurate quotation in every respect, except that Tennyson refused in his letter to write out any verses for

Bok, and his salutation "My dear young namesake" indicates clearly that Bok used the name "Alfred Tennyson Bok" in order to elicit a reply from the aging poet, always adamant in refusing his autograph to applicants. One pictures "Edward" as a youth, but he was actually nineteen years of age when in 1883 he tricked the old poet into writing to him. I called these facts to the attention of the late Judge Curtis Bok of Philadelphia, who, in a blustering letter, threatened to "take action" if I published my discovery. His opinion was that Tennyson either wrote "young namesake" in error, or else the letter I had was not the one sent to Bok.

Subsequently I discovered further evidence that Bok's *Autobiography* is not strictly factual. In it, he relates a story of meeting General and Mrs. Grant and showing them his autograph collection: "when he [Grant] came to a letter from General Sherman, Edward remembers that he chuckled audibly, reread it, and then turning to Mrs. Grant, said: 'Julia, listen to this from Sherman. Not bad.' The letter he read was this:

" 'Dear Mr. Bok:—

'I prefer not to make scraps of sentimental writing. When I write anything I want it to be real and connected in form, as for instance, in your quotation from Lord Lytton's play of 'Richelieu,' 'The pen is mightier than the sword' . . ." Now, Bok was in error about what Grant read, for this letter—and I have seen the original—was addressed to James Van Verder of Brooklyn, New York. Bok lived in Brooklyn, and I am pretty much convinced that there was no James Van Verder, but that the name was actually another of the aliases used by Bok in begging for autographs.

If Bok could, as he did, deliberately distort the facts pertaining to two letters in his autograph collection, one wonders just how much perversion of fact and even total fabrication there is in his goody-goody *Autobiography*. A great deal, I suspect, and certainly more than we would expect in a book which won the Pulitzer prize and was widely acclaimed by critics.

The adoption of aliases by manuscript usurers was not confined to Edward W. Bok. The late George Van Nosdall, a rabidly anti-Semitic rare-book and autograph dealer who holds the unenviable distinction of being the only confrère I ever threw out of my shop, simply used to badger noted authors. He used many aliases, but his favorite was *Kouti*. To his victims, comprising only those authors whose presentation volumes were readily saleable, he sent fulsome letters of praise, asking that they brighten his life by inscribing a book to him. As soon as he received a volume signed by his "favorite author," it would appear for sale in one of his mimeographed lists.

Van Nosdall's deception was not original. Nearly forty years ago, St. John Ervine wrote in the *Manchester Guardian* about the impositions practiced by Californians:

"A gentleman in California . . . wrote the following letter to me:

" 'For some time I have been collecting your first

editions, and during the past few months I have had the extreme pleasure of reading your following books:—

"'Charming Winds'

"'The Foolish Lovers'

"'The Wayward Man.'

"'All of these books I have in first English editions. I would appreciate, very much, an autograph inscription in your own handwriting. I hope you will not take this request in any other light than one who appreciates your works and would be much pleased to have your autograph.'

"Now, that, you would say, is very handsome of the gentleman. Surely, you will add, the recipient of so engaging a letter will not be churl enough to refuse to gratify his admirer with an autograph. But softly, sir or madam, as the case may be. I have not yet published the book called 'The Wayward Man.' It is not, in fact, finished. The gentleman has read somewhere a paragraph about the book and has mistaken a statement that it was about to be published for a statement that it has already been published. The gentleman has probably written to a score of authors in similar terms, begging for autographs, and may bag a few signed copies of books from innocent and flattered authors who have not yet discovered that there is a trade in autographed books in America conducted by booksellers who successfully cadge for signed copies from the writers.

"At one time authors received at regular intervals a letter purporting to come from a California banker, who began by asking the recipient of the letter if he would like to do a favour for a chubby, blue-eyed girl of two, his daughter, his only child. His ambition was to give her on her twenty-first birthday an album containing the signatures of all the distinguished people of his time. That album, even though it contained the signatures of popes and kings, statesmen and soldiers and sailors, men of letters and artists, would be incomplete if it did not also contain the signature of the recipient of the letter. Three years in succession that request came to me, and still the chubby, blue-eyed girl continued to be two years of age."

TRICKS OF THE TRADE

Collecting autographs can be an art, a profession, an investment or just plain fun. Whoever adventures into this romantic hobby will discover a whole new exhilarating world.

Here, out of four decades of experience, is advice for collectors with no funds at all and advice for millionaires, advice for those who are just beginning and for those who already have enjoyed many years of pleasant collecting.

17

THE RECKLESS MOTORIST WHO DROVE A STRANGE BARGAIN

The motor car veered suddenly off the road, as though out of control, and crashed violently into two newly planted saplings on the lawn of the beautiful estate at Bateman's in Burwash, Sussex, England. As the driver stepped from his car to survey the damage, he was confronted by an angry gardener to whom he apologized profusely.

"Here's my name and address," he said, handing his visiting card to the gardener. "If the owner will let me know the cost of replacing these trees, I'll post him a cheque at once."

Two days later the reckless motorist got the following letter:

"Dear Sir: My gardener tells me that it will cost three pounds to replace the two oak saplings, both of which were too badly injured to be saved. I should appreciate your cheque."

The letter was signed by the noted author, Rudyard

Kipling. But it went unanswered, until finally, three weeks later, Mr. Kipling renewed his request, in a more peremptory letter:

"I trust it will not be necessary for me to engage my solicitor to obtain from you the three pounds for the two trees destroyed."

The letter bore a large, bold signature of the world-famous poet and novelist.

This time the motorist replied:

"I am very sorry to have put you to so much inconvenience, Mr. Kipling, but I desperately wanted a letter from you in my autograph collection. I tried in every way possible to get one. I wrote to you almost a dozen times but got no reply. Forgive my subterfuge. You have made me a very happy collector, for I now possess two interesting letters from your pen. I thank you with all my heart . . .

"P.S. Here is a cheque in full payment for the trees."

When I read this story as a boy of twelve in Flint, Michigan, it stimulated my imagination. Although I had collected stamps and coins, cigar-bands, bread wrappers and even specimens of sand from various parts of the world (which I imagined would prove useful if I decided to become a detective), I had never hit upon the idea of assembling an autograph collection.

I had just finished reading Kipling's *Jungle Book*, a gift to me on my twelfth birthday; and the thought that I, too, might own a signature of the great Kipling seemed to me quite wonderful, especially since his autograph was so hard to get. Not knowing that Kipling was paid five dollars a word for everything he wrote, it occurred to me that if I were to send him ten cents, my weekly wages for hauling out our furnace ashes, it might help to overcome his distaste for autograph collectors.

I enclosed my dime with a letter that I still recall as clearly as the day I dropped it in the mailbox:

> Dear Mr. Kipling,
> I am a boy twelve years old. I read your Jungle Book all the way through and liked it very much because I like cobras and wolves.
> As I am starting an autograph collection I would like very much to have your signature to begin with as it is the hardest to get. I am enclosing ten cents to cover all costs. This dime is what I got paid for taking out the furnace ashes this week.
> > Your admirer,
> > CHARLES HAMILTON

I was prepared, of course, for the likelihood that I wouldn't hear from Mr. Kipling. After I mailed the letter, I began an eager vigil of the mailbox. Every morning before school I greeted the postman with an unaccustomed courtesy that must have disconcerted him. I wanted to make sure he delivered any mail, especially *the* mail, addressed to me. But as the days passed and no answer came, I gradually reconciled myself to the fact that Kipling was too preoccupied and too important to write his signature for a boy several thousand miles away. I finally stopped looking for the foreign stamp on an envelope with a return-address from England, and I returned ruefully to my stamps and coins and bread wrappers.

Then, one afternoon nearly six weeks later, long after I had given up hope, I came home from school and spotted a small envelope, propped up against the silver-plated cream jug on our dining-room sideboard. I noticed it at once because it bore a strange, brownish-red stamp and was addressed to Charles Hamilton, Esq., 526 East Fifth Street, Flint, Michigan, U.S.A.

Although I did not quite understand the abbreviation, *Esq.*, I knew it was a title of importance, and I presumed the letter was addressed to my father, whose name was the same as mine; but curiosity impelled me to take the envelope in my hands and turn it over. I read on the back flap the magic words: "Bateman's, Burwash, Sussex."

Opening the envelope and relishing the contents was one of the supreme thrills of my life. Inside was a typed note, "With Mr. Kipling's compliments," and, more important, a full signature of my favorite author. How I admired and fondled and studied that bit of paper. Not only had I succeeded where others had failed, but I was now granted the privilege (which I exercised endlessly) of holding and touching an authentic signature of the world's most famous writer. I had an autograph collection of one autograph!

From the moment I looked into that envelope both my lifelong hobby and career were decided. That signature of Kipling may have cost me a full week's salary, but it also changed the course of my life.

Inspired by this first success, I wrote to other men whom I admired. In quick succession I added to my collection the signatures of Thomas A. Edison and William Howard Taft. Scores of others followed. Soon I became dissatisfied with mere signatures and began to seek interesting letters. I wanted to read the ideas of these great

Rudyard Kipling

heroes of mine. Orville Wright sent me a signed photo-engraving of his first flight at Kitty Hawk. Clarence B. Kelland declined to give me a "sentiment," explaining, "I am not a sentimental person." Ellis Parker Butler wrote out a verse about his famous tale, "Pigs is Pigs":

"Pigs is pigs in Flushing
And pigs is pigs in Cork,
But pigs ain't pigs in butcher shops
'Cause there pigs is pork."

And he signed it with a bold signature and a sketch of a pig with a corkscrew tail.

John Philip Sousa told me how he happened to compose "The Stars and Stripes Forever": "The inspiration came to me as I was pacing the deck of a steamship on which I was returning to America some thirty years ago.

I hurried to my stateroom and set down the entire march in a few minutes." I asked Stephen Leacock, the Canadian humorist, how he got the ideas for his stories—was it while playing golf, or listening to a dull sermon in church, or after sitting for about ten hours thinking. He answered: "I can play golf but I can't think when I play it. I used to go to church—to have to go to church—so much when I was your age that I got a fund of thought out of it not yet exhausted. As for ten hours, make it ten seconds."

I wrote to Justice Oliver Wendell Holmes, Jr., then perhaps the greatest jurist in America, and asked him which of his father's poems he liked the best, expressing my own youthful preference for "The One Hoss Shay." He replied:

My dear boy,
Your question will have to go unanswered for several reasons, one of which is enough. I do not know. I think that you are right in liking 'The One Hoss Shay.'
Faithfully yours,
OLIVER WENDELL HOLMES, JR.

Vachel Lindsay was my favorite poet at the time, and I desperately wanted even a signature from his pen. But I wrote five letters without any response at all. Finally I hit upon the idea of a unique apology: "Dear Mr. Lindsay: I have written to you five times for your signature, but did not get it. I now wish to apologize for bothering you, as I have just learned from a friend that you never send your autograph because your wife forbids you to do it." By return mail I received a signed photograph and an autographed copy of his famous "Map of the Universe."

By the time I was fifteen I had accumulated an extensive, if not very valuable, collection. But there were also many failures. Hoover and Coolidge resisted my appeals. And the great George Bernard Shaw never yielded a penstroke to my blandishments. I later learned that, like many other celebrities, including Robert Louis Stevenson, Shaw seldom wrote collectors save in ire. Recently I sold a typically Shavian letter penned to an autograph hound who, after comparing his talents with William Blake's, requested the hot-tempered Irish dramatist to collaborate with him in writing lyrics for his correspondent's puerile music. Shaw could not resist the temptation to castigate his petitioner: "I am a very old man without many months to live. I cannot spare you '4 or 5' of them to do your business as well as my own. You must be an extraordinarily thoughtless person to make such a request. Your songs . . . a glance takes them in as simple little tunes without a single progression that would have surprised a baby in the XVIIth century. You have associated them with the great name of Blake instead of with Mary Had a Little Lamb. You have mistaken your size."

Quite often I am asked: "How did you get started as an autograph dealer?"

My career as a dealer began many years ago when, after a stint as an office manager, I began working as a

Charles Hamilton at age fifteen, already an enthusiastic collector and owner of a large but not very valuable collection of autographs.

free-lance copywriter and author. I had just finished reading an interesting article on Old John Brown by the distinguished historian and collector, Boyd B. Stutler, and it occurred to me that in my modest collection was a letter by an almost-forgotten abolitionist, predicting that Brown's hanging would trigger the Civil War. Since the letter had cost me only one dollar, my first thought was to present it to Mr. Stutler. Then, on a sudden whim, I decided I would offer it at his own price. I wrote to him, describing the letter and asking that he set a fair value. His reply was courteous and pleasant, but he pointed out, rather petulantly I thought, that "you, as the seller, should name the price."

My idea of the value was about five times what I had paid—five dollars. I presumed that Mr. Stutler's was approximately the same. But I was annoyed because, after I had taken the trouble to tell him about the letter, he had asked *me* to set the price. Was he not the expert on John Brown?

I sent a curt note that my price was fifty dollars. This would, I thought, end the matter. It did; but not as I expected, for by return mail I received a check for fifty dollars. This was nearly half of my weekly income at the time, and I was so amazed at the ease of my success that I decided to adventure upon a second endeavor.

In my collection was a letter by an obscure legislator, dated in 1816, discussing the property rights and sale of "the Old State House" in Philadelphia. I had bought the letter a few months earlier for fifty cents from Elmer

Heise, a Syracuse autograph dealer who specialized in inexpensive material. Possibly Heise had not realized that the Old State House was Independence Hall, the birthplace of American freedom. But I was aware of this fact, and I felt certain that the letter was worth ten times its cost.

"I'll offer this letter to the Historical Society of Pennsylvania," I told a friend. "They can name their own price and even if it's no more than a dollar—double what I paid—they can have it, for it truly belongs in their archives."

The answer to my offer was discouraging. The Society already had a large collection of material on Independence Hall, the date on my letter was very late, and the writer was insignificant, and—would I set the price?

There was no dodging the truth of the Society's observations. But, again, I failed to realize that I was becoming a professional and should have named the selling figure. I mistakenly believed that as experts they ought to have fixed the value.

I decided to close out my career as an autograph vendor by a single, bold impertinence. I wrote: "The price is $100." To my astonishment, the Society bought the letter.

Amazed by the ease with which I had sold these two letters, both purchased from dealers, at exactly one hundred times my cost, I decided to offer for sale a few other letters in my collection. They sold readily at prices much higher than I had paid. Thus, almost effortlessly, I made the difficult transition from amateur to professional.

In November, 1953, I put out my first slender catalogue, consisting entirely of autographs from my personal collection. It was a great success.

18

RARITIES FOR THE PRICE
OF A POSTAGE STAMP

Not long ago a young man came into my shop to sell a collection of *Time* magazine covers. Each cover was signed by its subject, and the youth displayed them with great pride and not a little arrogance.

"It's taken me over five years to build this collection," he announced with a complacent smile, "and I think you'll agree it's a remarkable one."

Yes, I had to agree. It *was* remarkable. Every cover, with a lurid portrait in *Time*'s pop style, had been creased and folded in the mails, so that portions of the glossy finish had cracked away. Although I didn't tell the young man, more than half of his covers were signed by secretaries or with Autopen (robot) signatures.

Here was a collection that had been assembled with no more expense to the owner than the cost of the magazines and the postage for mailing the covers. But how could I tell this young man outright that his treasured collection had little monetary value? I am frequently offered such collections. One man who wrote me, suggesting that I buy his rare collection of signed *Time* covers, observed that by tabulation there were only forty-five such collections in existence. That may be; but, if so, I must have been offered all forty-five of them! *Time* magazine recently commented on the fetish for collecting its signed covers, and praised collectors for their discrimination. I sent seven covers signed by Richard Nixon and seven signed by Robert F. Kennedy, all with machine signatures, to the editor. I explained that collectors of signed *Time* covers were getting not authentic autographs, but robot signatures of no value. I received a rather patronizing reply from the editor's secretary stating that the editor was well aware of this fact but did not choose to inform his subscribers. I wonder to whom he presented the Nixon and Kennedy robot signed covers which I sent him? Or possibly he added them to his own private collection of signed *Time* covers!

But the young man standing in my office, unlike many collectors, doubtless had no knowledge of collecting fads and probably had built half his future around the money he hoped to realize from his priceless gallery of currently venerated personalities. Yet his treasured collection had almost no value.

I thought of explaining to him that the signed covers weren't really in my field but I could suggest another dealer who would be interested. The alternative was to tell him honestly that his collection had practically no monetary worth. His callow assertiveness as he waited with his arms folded over his chest and with the trace of a smug smile lifting the corners of his mouth made up my mind.

"The collection would be worth fifteen dollars to me," I said.

"What!" he exclaimed. "Why, it's filled with famous names. Took me a lot of hard work to get them, too. Why, just look! Here's a cover signed by Douglas MacArthur."

I looked at the cover. True, it bore a genuine signature of MacArthur; but it was in deplorable condition— ragged and torn, with a large scuff mark through the signature of the famous general.

"MacArthur's signature is far from rare," I told him. "He lived a long life; and he invariably presented his signature to all those who requested it, including the thousands who plagued him with covers of *Time*. It's unfortunate that you didn't ask MacArthur to sign something more interesting than this dull, battered magazine cover, certainly worth no more than a few dollars to any collector.

"What do you mean by something more interesting?"

"Not long before MacArthur's death," I explained, "a young collector asked me for advice on what sort of autographic mementoes to collect from the outstanding World War II heroes. I told him: 'Use your imagination. Type out MacArthur's "Old soldiers never die" speech— or hand-letter it if you can't type—and get him to sign it. Ask him to sign a copy of the Japanese surrender treaty.

216

If you can afford a document of Hitler, buy one and see if you can't get Eisenhower to sign it. What a great document that would be—with the signatures of both Hitler and Eisenhower! Or perhaps you could get Admiral Doenitz, Hitler's successor who still lives in Germany, to sign the German surrender treaty to The Allied Powers.' "

"I see what you're getting at," said the young man, looking rather disconsolately at his collection of *Time* covers.

"Less than two years ago," I went on, I handled the very document I suggested that my friend try to get—obviously he had decided to take my advice, only he used *my* imagination—a typescript of the 'Instrument of Surrender,' Tokyo Bay, Japan, September 2, 1945, signed just before his death by MacArthur. I catalogued this fascinating document in one of my auction sales. It fetched $700.

"You see," I explained, "it's the historic interest of an autograph that gives it value. There is certainly nothing wrong with collecting signed *Time* covers, or autographed blocks of stamps, or first-day covers. They are interesting hobbies. But why go to all the trouble to get Salvador Dali to sign a block of Spanish stamps (which, with his signature, will be worth only about five dollars or ten dollars), when you could get him to sign a fascinating statement from his autobiography, or his opinion of Picasso, or even your own reconstruction of his famous mustache made from cornsilk!"

The young man packed up his collection of *Time*

covers. "I'm going to keep these as an object lesson," he said. "And from now on I'm going to use my imagination and gather colorful, interesting autographs."

One of my very good friends, the late Reverend Cornelius Greenway of Brooklyn, collected signed photographs of celebrities. On the surface, not a very exciting hobby, but the Reverend Greenway brought excitement to it. His photographs, for which he often spent several dollars, are beautifully done by famous news agencies, and generally depict the subject at a moment of great triumph or disaster. Connie would persuade the celebrity to write a comment or two on the photograph about the incident portrayed. The elusive Khrushchev, who rarely sends his autograph to Americans, was seduced into compliance when Connie sent him a photograph of the first Russian moon strike. The great Russian dictator affixed a large bold signature.

Congressman Seymour Halpern, who started his collection as a boy by asking celebrities to sign drawings of them rendered by his own talented pen, has now built a superb collection. One of his great successes as a youth came when he made a drawing of George Bernard Shaw, with the faint suggestion of horns on his head, and sent it to the aging dramatist for a signature. "Have I deserved this?" wrote Shaw beneath it, adding a bold autograph. Even the elusive Sir Arthur Conan Doyle yielded to Halpern's artistry, writing under a sketch, "As I am over 70 I don't think this is very accurate. However you have made the best of a bad job."

Recently, Congressman Halpern was discussing his collection with me. He asked me if I could suggest any improvements.

"Since you are a friend of President Johnson," I said, "why not ask him to sign the Presidential oath of office for you? It would be a great historic treasure."

A few months later, while Seymour and his lovely wife, Barbara, were chatting over dinner with my wife and me, the Congressman suddenly burst out with the question, "Guess what I just added to my collection?"

I declined to speculate, and Seymour explained: "I was with the President and his staff, flying in the very plane in which Johnson took the oath of office after the murder of Kennedy. I asked Johnson's secretary if she would type for me the Presidential oath of office on a sheet of the plane's stationery. She was kind enough to do it for me. Then I asked Johnson, who was sitting at his plane desk, 'Would you mind signing this for me, Mr. President?' He studied it very carefully, then said, 'I don't know whether I should do this—oh, well . . .' and put a bold signature at the bottom. 'This is the first and only Presidential oath of office I ever signed,' he added. 'The others were verbal and no signature was called for.'"

What is this great treasure, on which the ink is barely dry, worth? It is unique, and someday, hundreds of years hence, will be enshrined in some great archive or library.

And, since my friend Seymour seems to have a way with Lyndon B. Johnson, I feel sure that he can persuade him to write on a document signed by President Andrew

Johnson a statement as to whether the two Presidents are related. Imagine! The same document signed by two Presidents of the same name who were President exactly a century apart!

Almost any intelligent collector able to spend a few hours and a few cents postage each week on his hobby can build an important and worthwhile collection merely by using his imagination. If you write to your favorite author, you might ask him pertinent questions about his books, or how he happened to start as an author, or the one sentence of advice he would give to aspiring writers. The noted collector of the middle of the nineteenth century, Lewis J. Cist of Cincinnati, spent many years in gathering his collection of poems written out by celebrated authors. Even Francis Scott Key penned *The Star-Spangled Banner* for Cist, a manuscript which cost the collector only three cents in postage but is today worth at least $50,000.

Many autograph seekers believe that a letter must be signed by a celebrity in order to be valuable. Not so. Recently I sold at auction a dictated document of Biuku Gasa, one of the rescuers of Lieutenant John F. Kennedy after the sinking of his PT-109 in World War II. Biuku described the rescue, and his statement fetched $600 because of its great historic interest.

Lying before me as I write is an unpublished letter (1958) of Philip Diamant, a soldier who served under Captain Dwight D. Eisenhower in World War I. Diamant writes:

Captain Eisenhower's sense of humor was clearly shown when the boys painted my bald head. It was Friday and we had returned from a 20-mile hike and I was tired out so, after supper, I shaved and went to sleep. It was while I slept that the boys painted Sunny Jim on my head. The face was painted so that it showed a smile and one tooth. The next day was Saturday and as I had very little hair I did not use a mirror when I washed my face, therefore I was ignorant of the picture on top of my head. After breakfast, the usual Saturday inspection was held for equipment and as I stood at the foot of my bunk Eisenhower came along and he looked at me, stood for a moment, and asked, 'Are you coming or going?' . . . I did not answer as I did not know what he was talking about, but thought that the heat had gotten my captain as it was extremely warm, and he also had a slight grin on his face as he left the barracks.

I was still wondering what he meant by the remark of "are you coming or going" when a few minutes later a runner . . . entered the barracks and told me to report to the captain in the orderly room.

Ike looked at me and then handed me a trench mirror and what I saw made me burst out in a fit of laughter. He also had a smile as he said, "Here is a three-day pass to New York with transportation paid. Now you go back and have a good laugh on those boys in the barracks."

Imagine the fascination of a collection of letters, penned by unknowns, describing incidents in the lives of great men! How much more interesting would such an assemblage be than a mere drab accumulation of signatures on cards.

Recently I received a letter from a young man who asked a question frequently put to me: "What is the best way to compose a letter requesting signatures and photographs?"

If this youth proposes a collection of signatures—mere scraps of evidence that a celebrity knows how to write his name—I should urge him to reconsider. Except for a few rarities, like Washington and Lincoln, such scrawls on paper or cards have, as a rule, very little or no value. I sell them in lots of hundreds at my auctions. On the other hand, a collection of *letters* or *documents* which explain or illuminate the literature or history of the world will always be of value and will be a delight to look at and study.

As for composing a letter to a celebrity, my suggestion is to learn something about him first—look into his life and achievements. Then, if you are really interested and want to know him better, write openly and honestly to him, and ask him a question or make a request in such a way that it will take only a few moments of his time to answer. Don't worry about the way you phrase your letter. Just be honest, and you will probably be successful.

Some collectors resort to a strange technique in order to extract a letter from a celebrity. Like the angler who goes after a wary, well-fed trout, they irritate him by casting a lure under his nose until he strikes. George Bernard Shaw always fell for such tricks. He could never resist castigating a minister pleading for funds. John Ruskin rose to the same bait. To a reverend who solicited a loan for a church he wrote: "Starve and go to heaven —but don't borrow. Try first begging—I don't mind, if

COMPOSER

QUEEN

NOVELIST

TYRANT

EMPEROR

CONDUCTOR

DICTATOR

PRESIDENT

NAVAL OFFICER

POET

EXPLORER

MADMAN

ARTIST

"Saints and Sinners!"

How many of the famous people—whose signatures appear
above — can you identify?

(See over for correct answers)

COMPOSER

NOVELIST

EMPEROR

DICTATOR

NAVAL OFFICER

EXPLORER

QUEEN

TYRANT

CONDUCTOR

PRESIDENT

POET

MADMAN

ARTIST

LEFT (top to bottom): Frederic Chopin, Charles Dickens, Napoleon, Mussolini, John Paul Jones, Christopher Columbus.

RIGHT (top to bottom): Mary (Queen of Scots), Ivan the Terrible, Arturo Toscanini, John F. Kennedy, Lord Byron, Adolf Hitler, Toulouse-Lautrec.

it's really needful, stealing. But don't buy things you can't pay for. And of all manner of debtors, pious people building churches they can't pay for are the most detestable nonsense to me. Can't you preach and pray behind the hedges—or in a sandpit—or in a coal hole first?" This precious letter, worth far more than the modest cash contribution Ruskin might have sent, immediately took an honored place in the collector's portfolio.

Sometimes valuable letters are obtained under similar but more pleasant circumstances. When Prince Alexander of Battenberg, then a schoolboy, ran out of pocket-funds, he wrote to his sedate grandmother, Queen Victoria, asking for financial help. He received no money but a rebuke in the form of a letter enjoining him to use his allowance more wisely in the future. To this he replied: "My dear Grandmama, I am sure you will be glad to know that I need not trouble you for any money just now, for I sold your last letter to another boy here for thirty shillings."

19

THE ART OF BUYING FROM DEALERS

"Hurry," I cried to my secretary. "I want to send a straight cable to England."

Only a few minutes earlier, the postman had brought me an English catalogue. I had looked at every item listed, reading swiftly, but was quite captivated by the description of a magnificent letter of the great ornithologist, John J. Audubon, entirely about his famous work, *The Birds of America*. The price was only five pounds—less than fifteen dollars.

Within thirty seconds my cable was on its way. Three days later the Audubon letter reached me by airmail, with a note from the British dealer saying that my cable was the first of fifteen to request this rare letter.

In my shop when it arrived was Robert K. Black, the well-known New Jersey dealer. I told him of my good fortune and he asked, "What do you want for it?"

"Well, I paid fourteen dollars. A profit of one hundred dollars would satisfy me."

Black snapped it up, almost with the same eagerness I

Doris Harris,
San Pedro, Calif.

Mary A. Benjamin,
Walter R. Benjamin Autographs,
New York.
Seated is her husband, the noted
Oriental scholar, Harold E. Hen-
derson.

Paul C. Richards,
Brookline, Mass.

Robert K. Black,
Upper Montclair, New Jersey

Rosejeanne Slifer,
New York, N.Y.

Bruce Gimelson,
Fort Washington, Penna.

Gordon T. Banks,
Goodspeed's Book Shop,
Boston, Mass.

King V. Hostick,
Springfield, Illinois

David Kirschenbaum (center)
Carnegie Book Shop,
New York, N.Y.

Dr. Rudolf F. Kallir
(collector-dealer)
New York, N.Y.

Mabel Zahn,
Charles Sessler, Inc.,
Philadelphia, Penna.

Kenneth W. Rendell,
Kingston Galleries, Inc.,
Somerville, Mass.

Conway Barker,
La Marque, Texas

Dr. Milton Kronovet,
Brooklyn, New York

Maury A. Bromsen,
Maury A. Bromsen Associates,
Boston, Mass.

had, and within a few days he had sold it at a fine advance.

During the past twenty years I have made more than half a million dollars by buying from other dealer's catalogues. I follow these simple principles, here set down for the first time:

—*Read catalogues the moment they arrive.* Even seconds are precious when you seek desirable items. A man who understood the science of ordering was the late Dr. Max Thorek. I once had a hurried—and successful—order from Dr. Thorek, who had read my catalogue while walking down the hospital corridor from one room to another in each of which he was scheduled to perform a major operation; and even as he phoned, his second patient was being anaesthetized.

—*Order instantly by phone or telegram.* Important and interesting catalogues are often out-of-date within twenty-four hours after they are issued. Try to get them sent to you by airmail.

—*Never assume any item is sold; always order it.* A few years ago I ordered a pair of letters of Conan Doyle about Sherlock Holmes from a French catalogue so ancient that the paper was already turning brown. I had no idea of the age of the catalogue, only that it had taken three weeks to reach me from Southern France. The price for the two letters was just thirty-five dollars, a ridiculously low sum, and although I was certain some alert collector had long ago snapped them up, I cabled to Nice for them. The letters came to me by airmail and I sold them at once for somewhat more than ten times what I had paid.

—*Get catalogues from as many dealers as possible.* By examining the catalogues of half-a-dozen or more dealers, you will soon learn which dealers are reasonable and which are expensive. Never, however, refuse to buy a really significant and desirable

230

autograph merely because the price is high. How many "high" prices of yesterday now look like incredible bargains!

I once bought a small and undistinguished collection of autographs, among which was a manuscript signed "Rose Greenhow," describing an espionage adventure during the Civil War. So rare is the autograph of this celebrated Confederate spy that I had never seen an example of it. I labelled it as a clerical copy and priced it at five dollars. Robert K. Black discovered it among my recent acquisitions.

"You can have it for three dollars and fifty cents," I told him.

He bought it, and a few days later at lunch he said to me. "I think that the Rose Greenhow is an *original manuscript* in her hand." He pulled it from his brief case. "Here! See what you think."

Black had amassed considerable evidence to prove his point and I blushed heartily to discover that he had purchased a very valuable manuscript from me for a fraction of its worth.

"Well," I told him. "You've caught me in a blunder. Now I want to buy it back. How much?"

"Cheap to you," he said, smiling. "Only ten times what I paid."

I cheerfully gave Bob Black thirty-five dollars. Although I felt the manuscript was really worth upwards of $500, when I came to offer it to James N.B. Hill, the noted collector of espionage autographs, I decided that

Bob's markup was more proper under the circumstances, and sold the precious document for $350. Today it would certainly fetch upwards of $1000 at auction.

I have sold many a bargain in my career. The list of my pricing indiscretions is too long to chronicle here, but I might mention one example because I thought at the time that I was making a big profit. A scout, one of those evanescent gentlemen who makes a living searching the countryside for rarities, brought me a somewhat battered and frayed document signed by Peyton Randolph, the Virginia patriot. I glanced at it, and saw to my astonishment that it was nothing less than a list of the actual terms by which the State of Virginia agreed to approve the United States Constitution in 1788. The Virginians demanded a "bill of rights," and set down more than twenty provisions, ten of which subsequently became the first ten amendments to the Constitution.

"What do you want for it?" I asked.

"Would $300 be okay?"

I said that I would pay that sum, and the scout left with my check. No doubt he had picked the document up for a few dollars.

That night I examined the old paper, tenderly straightening out the creases as I read it. I was enjoying my evening manhattan and priced the document at exactly twice what I had paid—$600. By the time I finished the drink, however, my sense of drama was awakened and I decided that, after all, $900 was a more appropriate price.

I mixed myself a second manhattan, and the full rarity of the document suddenly dawned upon me. Here was an extraordinary piece of Americana, the actual draft of the Bill of Rights. Certainly it was worth $1200, if it was worth a cent, and I erased my earlier price to replace it with the new figure.

The second drink brought with it a wave of patriotic fervor. I read the document again, carefully weighing each of its immortal words. It was not merely a preliminary Bill of Rights—it was a credo of American freedom. Here, on this very paper before me, were the ideals and hopes of the men of the Revolution.

I erased the price again—the paper was getting a bit thin—and increased it to $1500.

By the time I finished my second manhattan (it must have been a powerful one!) I knew that I could not part with this precious bit of America's heritage for less than $2500. And that is the price at which I sold it the next day to a Chicago collector. What is such a great document really worth? Would $25,000 be too much?

If, at times, you lose patience with a dealer because his catalogue does not reach you faster and the choicest items are sold, or because he failed to describe a tiny tear in the corner of a letter, or because he underpriced or overpriced a document, remember that he, too, has many problems.

Some collectors, admittedly, are very trying. Once I offered in a catalogue a holograph poem signed by William Cullen Bryant. One of my customers telephoned, saying that he was very interested, and could I read the poem to him over the phone.

I declaimed eloquently, stanza after stanza, to the very end.

"Splendid," said my customer. "Send it along. I'll take it."

A few days later it came back with the laconic comment, "Not the poem I thought it was."

On another occasion I offered a printed funeral march commemorating the death of Abraham Lincoln.

A customer phoned. "I'll take that march," he said seriously, "but only if Lincoln signed it."

Collectors often pit their knowledge against the dealer with great success. Occasionally, however, inexperienced customers decided to tilt with the expert and the results are often very amusing. Once a collector whom I barely knew offered me in trade a "signed" photograph of Stephen Collins Foster. The photo was a cabinet reproduction made about 1870, and the signature was an obvious forgery.

I informed the collector of my conclusions.

"It so happens," he said haughtily, "that I have studied this signature carefully and know it to be genuine."

I told him that the cabinet photograph as an art form was not introduced into this country until 1865, the year after Foster's death. Thus, aside from the fact that the signature was a shaky copy of a well-known facsimile, it could not possibly be genuine.

CHARLES HAMILTON
AUTOGRAPHS, Inc.

OLD
MANUSCRIPTS
BOUGHT

5.3

"Mr. Breger" cartoon by Dave Breger.

"You must take my word for it that it is genuine," he insisted.

"What is your profession, sir?" I asked, changing the subject.

He said he was a doctor.

"Well, doctor," I said. "You have been so helpful and courteous in advising me without charge that I want you to know, in case you run into any difficult problems, you can count upon my help in giving you medical advice."

He burst out laughing, and a few minutes later had accepted my opinion on the "signed" photograph of Foster.

Once you begin purchasing from dealers and at auction, your name and collecting interests will quickly become known to dealers and librarians. If you are not unreasonable in your demands, and few collectors are, dealers will be delighted to assist you in the search for letters and documents which will add piquancy and importance to your collection. You will find yourself in the tight little fraternity of collectors, an amiable band that encircles the world. During World War II, when I was a sergeant, I was ferreting my way along the *bouquinistes* on the Left Bank in Paris with a friend, when a youth of about twelve approached us.

"My father would like you to visit our library," he said in French.

We accompanied the boy across the street, and entered with some bewilderment a baroque structure with a cavernous series of rooms filled with paintings, busts, and statues. A short, affable man, who spoke no English, greeted us. I introduced myself and my friend.

We talked briefly of old manuscripts and rare books, and when I mentioned the Gutenberg Bible, the librarian's face ignited with pleasure and he said, "You mean the *Mazarin* Bible."

Suddenly it occurred to me that we were in the famed Mazarin library, named after that great cardinal and collector of precious manuscripts and books who first identified the Gutenberg Bible and established its rarity. The gentleman to whom I was speaking was one of the most distinguished librarians in the world.

As we chatted I caught sight of a bust of Camoëns, the great Portuguese poet. I observed to our host that I was particularly interested in the *Lusiads*, Camoëns' famed epic of the voyage of Vasco da Gama, and had made a special study of the translations into English and French.

He joyously threw his arms around me. I felt like a soldier being embraced by the Emperor Napoleon. He too was a lover of the *Lusiads*. Moreover, he averred that most of the quasi-literates who visited the library had never heard of Camoëns and could not possibly have recognized the bust of the man with only one eye.

"What can I do for you?" he asked. "Our facilities are at your disposal. Tell me what rarities you would like to look at? I shall be delighted to serve you."

I am sure he expected me to ask for a view of the *Mazarin* Bible.

"We should like to look at," I said, speaking also for my friend, whose French was even more halting than mine, "the earliest known illustrated edition of that delectable poet, François Villon."

"Our rarest and most precious volume!" cried the old man. And he led us through a maze of safes and vaults and finally I had the enormous pleasure of holding in my hands one of my favorite books in all literature, in the very print and format in which it was born into the world.

20

HOW TO BID AT AUCTION

The first time you attend an auction you may be amazed by its explosive speed, with seemingly invisible bids flying at the auctioneer and his spotters from every part of the gallery. You may wonder how you can participate in any battle so subtle, with the floor bidders often as crafty and elusive as Indians, signalling their bids by the crook of a finger or the wiggle of an ear, and at times even dodging behind pillars or retreating almost out of the gallery so that their competitors will not know they are taking part in the fray.

Don't be afraid of the mystery of this struggle for rare letters and manuscripts. But be careful. You may find it a sport so exhilarating that it becomes a habit.

To bid at auction you need nothing more than the funds to pay for what you buy—or try to buy. The catalogue of a reliable auction house describes, usually in detail, every separate lot being offered. If the house guarantees what it sells, you can bid with confidence. Read carefully the terms of sale in front of the catalogue before you bid. If there is no guarantee, and material is offered "as is" or "at the buyer's risk," be sure to employ a dealer to bid for you unless you are an expert at autographs. The dealer's ten percent charge for his services is a bargain.

The correctness of description in an auction catalogue is of great importance, especially for mail bidders. Our executive vice president and cataloguer, H. Keith Thompson, Jr., insists upon accurate cataloguing. This reminds me of an amusing story. In the fall of 1966, when I sold the great collection of Lucius S. Ruder, I catalogued personally some of the more unusual lots, one of which was an ancient Sumerian clay tablet, still preserved with its original clay envelope. I described it as "expertly cracked so that the envelope may be removed to show the entire face of the encased tablet." The real story behind my painstaking cataloguing later came to light when Gordon T. Banks, the prominent autograph dealer of Goodspeed's in Boston, wrote in *Manuscripts:* "I sold this and other Sumerian items to Lucius Ruder and he prized this particular example very largely because by means of the cracked cover one could demonstrate the whole of this type of cuneiform and the method of preserving the secrecy of the content. At the time I told Mr. Ruder how this was so expertly cracked. One fall day I took the cuneiform to Harvard for a reading by a visiting German expert, and on my return by subway from Cambridge to Boston, I must have bumped against the turnstile for when I unwrapped the cuneiform in the office the clay envelope, or case, had been unconsciously 'expertly' cracked."

At my sales, all autographs are guaranteed genuine for my lifetime, and they may be returned if found to be other than described. Pre-sale estimates for guidance are printed right in the catalogue. Most other auction houses will furnish estimates on request, so that one will have a guide to the value. Of course, autographs often bring a fraction of the estimate or many times the estimate.

Several years ago I was offered a letter of Jacqueline Kennedy for which the English vendor asked a cash payment. It was a remarkable letter in which the First Lady replied from Palm Springs, on January 10, 1955, to a stranger who had asked her for $20,000:

> I received your letter and it has made me most unhappy these past few days. How wonderful it would be if this were a world where £7000 or $20,000 were merely to me the sum spent on an evening party as you put it. If that were true I would give what I could to enable you and your family to start a new life . . . The word millionaire has a magic ring to it, but I think there are probably left in the world only a few maharajahs who can throw money around like that.
>
> I could not possibly give you that amount of money, were you my closest friend or relative. True my husband is well-off, but taxes in this country are enormous . . . and when he has paid for the household expenses, and his business expenses . . . there is not just a great pile of money lying around, as you imagine . . .
>
> I explain all this to you, because I know it is hard to read about people who are rich when you are not, and I do not want you to think us spoiled and heartless. From your letter I think you

have something that a great many rich people don't have, and would give their fortune to acquire, a wife and family who adore you and whom you love . . .

I would have helped you if I could. I hate to put an end to your dream, but I think you were hoping for a miracle that just won't happen in the twentieth century . . . I am sure God will be kind to you.

At the time I was offered this letter, Mrs. Kennedy was still the First Lady. I had never handled any of her letters and had no great enthusiasm about them or confidence in their value. I sent sixty dollars for it. The owner replied that he thought the letter was worth eighty dollars and would I please mail him another twenty dollars. I read his reply to Robert K. Black, the Upper Montclair, New Jersey, rare book and autograph dealer, who was sitting across from my desk when I received it.

"If you would like me to pay that additional twenty dollars for a fourth-interest in Mrs. Kennedy's letter," said Black, who had read her reply to the begging stranger, "I'll be glad to."

"Fine!" I answered. "But don't blame me if you lose."

A few weeks later President Kennedy was assassinated, and a reporter from the *New York Herald Tribune*, Earl L. Talbott, dropped in to see me. He asked what Kennedy material I was going to sell at auction, and I suddenly thought of the Mrs. Kennedy letter, then buried in a large file on my desk.

Earl wrote the letter up in his Sunday column and

Bidders, spectators and newsmen at a Hamilton autograph auction. H. Keith Thompson, Jr., spotting bids for the auctioneer, stands at extreme left.

Gregory Mozian, auctioneer, in action

within a week it was famous, quoted in many magazines and newspapers.

Instead of the estimate of $150 which I intended to put on the letter, I made it $250. I figured the publicity had upped the value.

I sat open-mouthed at the sale as the price mounted rapidly beyond $250. The gallery crackled with excitement. A chic, attractive young lady, reputedly an agent of the Kennedys, was engaged in a fearful struggle for the ownership of the letter with an "invisible man" in the rear. A signal which I could not see reached the auctioneer.

"I have nine hundred dollars!"

"Nine hundred and fifty dollars!" said the chic woman.

The auctioneer glanced to the back of the gallery. "One thousand dollars," he cried.

The chic lady rose dramatically to her feet, took a blank check from her purse, tore it up, and walked out of the room.

But the bidding went on, and on, and on. When the letter was finally knocked down at the world-record price of $3000, the audience burst into applause.

Later, in commenting jocularly on my error in estimating the value of the letter, Black said to me: "Easiest seven hundred and thirty dollars I ever made."

The successful bidder, a Boston attorney who had never before bid at an autograph auction, told members of the press: "I drove down from Boston just to get this letter because I liked what it said. I had no idea what I was going to pay for it. I just played it by ear."

Despite my misjudgment of the value in this case, generally my estimates, and those of other reputable auction houses, come within twenty or thirty percent of the actual sum fetched.

Once you decide to try your luck at tilting, you will find it an easy matter to bid merely by raising your hand or your catalogue. This is the commonest type of signal, and even many well-known and skilled dealers use it. The auctioneer will let you know very clearly whether he has your bid, or that of another person, merely by saying, "The bid is in the front, on the right," or "The bid I have is that of the gentleman in the fourth row." If you should accidentally bid against yourself, something which even experienced bidders do, the auctioneer will let you know by saying, "The bid I have is yours, sir."

If you are a new bidder, unknown to the auction galleries, you may be asked to make a deposit. It is always a good idea to speak to the auctioneer or one of his assistants before the sale and let them know that you intend to bid. If you furnish adequate references you will not be asked for a deposit.

Every auction has its comic moments. Not long ago a bidder at one of the big galleries in New York lost his wallet during the excitement of the sale. He spoke to the auctioneer, who announced that a wallet containing $2000 had been lost in the room, and there was a reward of $200 for its return.

"$225" came a reward bid from the rear.

If you cannot attend the auction in person, you will find it just as safe and easy to bid by mail. There is no charge for executing your mail bids; but, if you prefer, you can get a dealer to bid for you.

In the back of each auction catalogue is a bid sheet. You simply write down the number of the lot or item in the left column, and the top amount you wish to bid on it in the right. Your bid or bids are then entered in an "order book," and the auctioneer's assistant will bid for you competitively against other mail bidders and against the bidders on "the floor," or in the auction room.

The usual progression of bids is as follows: by raises of two dollars and fifty cents to $25; by five dollars raises to $100; by ten dollar raises to $200; by twenty-five dollar raises to $1000.

Here is the way mail bids are executed at the sale. Suppose you have bid forty-five dollars on a lot estimated at forty-five dollars. Another mail bidder may submit a bid of twenty-five dollars. These two bids, twenty-five dollars and forty-five dollars, are entered in the order book. The bidding in the auction room opens at thirty dollars, which is the amount you must bid to beat the twenty-five dollar bidder. If there is no further bid from the audience, the lot is sold to you at thirty dollars. If a bidder in the room signals to the auctioneer that he will go higher, the auctioneer calls out, "I have thirty-five dollars!" The assistant with the order book says, forty dollars!" (He is bidding for you, and you have authorized him to bid as high as forty-five dollars.) If there is no further bid from the floor, the lot is knocked down to you at forty dollars, but if there is another floor bid, the assistant with the order book cries out, "Tie with the book!" The auctioneer then asks the room bidders to break the tie by going to fifty dollars. If no bidder in the room will advance to fifty dollars, the lot becomes yours at forty-five dollars, because, in the event of a tie, your mail bid has priority over the floor bid.

There is still another great advantage to mail bidders, not enjoyed by bidders who are present at the sale. All mail bids are confidential, and successful mail bidders do not have their names called out in the room. Instead, the auctioneer merely announces, "Sold to order."

Almost invariably, the really desirable, important, and exciting autographs are sold at auction, rather than through dealer's catalogues. That is why most collectors, sooner or later, turn to auctions. If you enjoy owning the truly beautiful and rare in the field of autographs, then you will find auctions a major source for building your collection.

And there is always the lurking possibility—I could cite hundreds of cases—of getting an autograph letter or document for a mere fraction of its value. I once bought a rare Aztec manuscript from Christie's of London for only $120. Several years later, after properly cataloguing and describing it, I sold it at auction in New York for $5,500.

I certainly hope that you will have similar good fortune; but, even if you don't, you will find auction bidding one of the most exciting of all games.

21

THE THRILL OF THE AUCTION ROOM

The auctioneer had cried his last lot. The glittering chandeliers in the great gallery were dark. Another sale was over. As I sat celebrating its success with a group of friends in my hotel suite, a waiter arrived with a tray of drinks. I remembered him vaguely as one who had served in our rooms several times before. But now he seemed woeful looking and I suspected he had just received bad news.

"Anything wrong?" I asked.

"Yes," he answered, with a touch of bitterness in his tone. "I was the underbidder tonight on the Napoleon document."

In my more than forty years in the autograph field I have often seen collectors go daft over a bit of paper bearing the signature of a famous person. I have watched men who a few minutes before would have scoffed at the idea of autograph collecting flush with excitement as they held in their hands an actual letter penned by Washington or Lincoln. Yet I must admit that I was startled by the waiter's remark. He did not seem to be the sort of man who would be swept away by the excitement of the auction floor. Nor did his occupation suggest that he might be a student of history.

"Why don't you join us in a drink?" I suggested. "And tell me what happened."

"I got a copy of your catalogue just before the sale," he explained, as he sipped a Scotch and soda, "and I glanced through it, almost without interest. In a vague sort of way, I knew that people collected autographs, but I considered them a bit on the nutty side.

"Well, as I was thumbing through the pages, reading about people I'd never heard of, I lit on your description of a Napoleon document. I read it three or four times before I realized I was getting very excited. The idea of owning an original document, one that Napoleon had really touched and looked at and even written his name on—that thrilled me. I know quite a bit about Napoleon and I've read many books about him. As I went about my work here at the hotel, I decided that it would be a great adventure to own an original Napoleon document.

"I am a family man, with a wife and children, and on my salary I really can't afford to put out the seventy dollars at which you estimated the Napoleon document. My wife would murder me if I spent that much on an old piece of paper. Still, I know that sometimes lots at auction go for less than your estimate, so I decided to take a fling. My heart was really pounding when the bidding opened on the Napoleon.

"The auctioneer started at forty dollars, and when I called out forty-five I was sure that every man and woman in the room was my enemy. But I also felt very courageous. All of a sudden Napoleon himself had inspired me!

"Then someone said fifty, and I tried to see who was bidding against me. And jump by jump the bids kept mounting, until I actually heard myself bid one hundred dollars. Boy, I was scared! I knew I couldn't go any higher. I heard the auctioneer say, 'going, going . . .' But just as he was about to let me have the document, a man in front of me raised his pencil. The auctioneer looked at me as he asked for one hundred and twenty. I was so frozen with excitement that I couldn't even shake my head. The other bidder became the owner at one hundred and ten dollars. I was at the same time relieved and crushed. Relieved, because I could not afford to pay one hundred dollars for the document, and crushed because I had lost a treasure."

I couldn't help feeling sorry for the waiter. "There will be other Napoleons," I consoled him. "Meanwhile, join us in another drink and we'll talk about Napoleon."

To those who will never know the excitement and exhilaration of the auction room, the thrills which our waiter discovered that evening, I offer my sympathy. To me the battles for ownership which take place on the gallery floor are fully as exciting as the struggles for disputed territory in war, and I have participated in both. But in the auction room there is great intrigue. And the intrigue deepens almost in direct ratio to the rarity and value of the manuscript being sold and the assets of those who are bidding for it. Some participants feign indifference, then suddenly burst in with their bids, hoping to intimidate or discourage their opponents and put them to rout. Others violently stab the air with their pencils. Many bid furtively, with eye-winks, twitches, or adjustments of the necktie. A few lose their nerve and wilt quickly in the face of the opposition. Others grow in audacity as the bidding gets heated and brazenly cry out their bids.

And there are the sly meetings before the sale, when dealers, seeking bargains, agree with each other to "lay off this lot if you'll lay off that" (strictly illegal.)

For the average collector, however, the auction will always remain *the* supreme experience. He pits his skill and ingenuity against titans and, on rare occasions, emerges triumphant.

One of the most dramatic auctions ever held, branded by some "a circus" or "a carnival" was the last sale I conducted at the once elegant Gotham Hotel. The sale had received wide publicity because I was offering letters of both Jacqueline Kennedy and Lee Harvey Oswald, a strange and quite accidental juxtaposition which delighted scholars and historians but horrified sentimentalists. The gallery was crowded with bidders, spectators, reporters and cameramen.

There was a plump woman in blue eye-shadow who had come to heckle. When the letters of Oswald came up

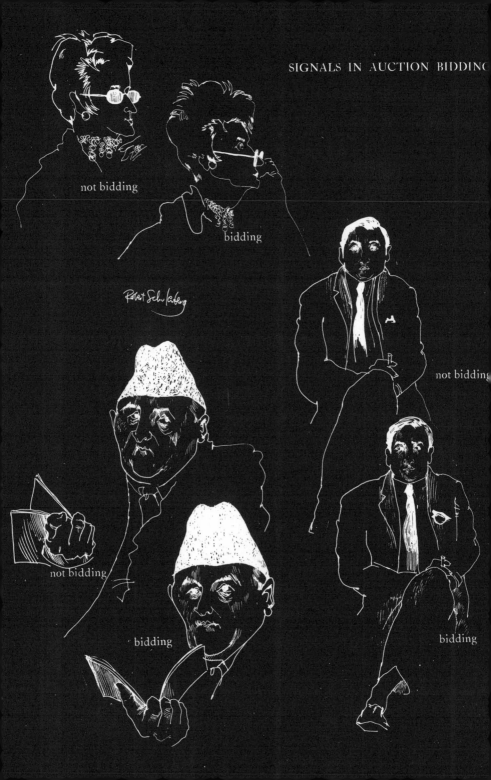

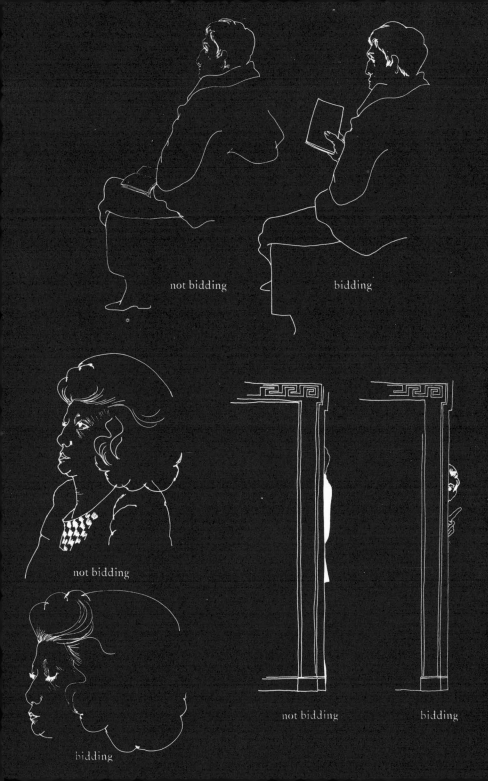

not bidding

bidding

not bidding

bidding

not bidding

bidding

for sale—they sold for a total of $7165—she rose dramatically, faced the television cameras, and orated in a voice loud enough to fracture the chandeliers, "I wouldn't give you a dollar for them." At the time, I thought perhaps she did not have a dollar to give, but later I learned from a reporter that she was a professional heckler who specialized in disrupting stockholder meetings.

The Gotham Hotel also decided to get in on the publicity by passing out circulars in the ballroom they had rented to me:

"The Gotham Hotel management doesn't approve of Charles Hamilton auctioning the Mrs. Jacqueline Kennedy and Lee Harvey Oswald letters. The hotel considers their being auctioned in bad taste. It wasn't aware that they would be auctioned when Mr. Hamilton rented the ballroom."

A television reporter asked me for a statement on the Gotham Hotel's circular. "If they were as eager to improve their service as they are to improve my taste," I said, "they'd have a great hotel."

Oddly, nobody has ever protested when I sell at auction the letters and documents of Hitler and his henchmen. The leading collectors of Nazi items are Jewish. An anomaly, perhaps, but it shows the fascination of evil. And just as the monstrous career of Hitler intrigues us, so does the career of Lee Harvey Oswald—and his letters.

It was a great sale for historians and scholars who saw

is, but everything is normal, right down to June's little fingernails.

I don't think we'll be at this address much longer so it is not advisable for you to write here.

The reason for the delay in some letters and the speed in others is because of the Russian censor who reads all letters.

I was not aware you sent other letters to me in the Hotel when I lived in Moscow and I left there for Minsk after I wrote that letter.

I cannot say where we shall go at first probably directly to Vernon.

Love
Lee

Last page of Lee Harvey Oswald letter which sold for $3000.

important documents bring high prices. And it was a bad sale for all those who sought to suppress historic facts and prevent historic documents from being sold. The sale of the Oswald and Mrs. Kennedy letters proved, once and for all, that Americans will not tolerate emotional censorship, and that all significant letters or documents, regardless of when or by whom penned, will receive the attention of the scholar.

Of course, manuscript auctions don't merely help scholars and historians. They also stimulate collectors, many of whom seek to preserve the written records of our nation. I recollect about two years ago that a four-teen-year-old boy came to see me just before a sale. The auction bacillus had got into his blood stream and he was eager to bid on an important letter of Franklin D. Roosevelt. He had very little money, but was willing to pledge his allowance for a year. I was touched by his earnestness and readily agreed to allow him a year to pay, in case his bid was successful. The letter which he sought of his hero, a typewritten letter signed, protested a smear story about Roosevelt's lameness. "That kind of story is so typically yellow-journalish that it creates a wholly false picture . . . the boat story is made out of whole cloth," wrote the future President in 1932. "The losing of my balance and toppling is not true. I wear a leg brace to lock the knee and on one occasion, when I was speaking, the brace broke with the result that I went half way down. Frankly, I cannot see the importance of all this nonsense when I am in perfect health and get through three times as much work in the course of the average day as three ordinary men do. Come up here and watch me for twenty-four hours . . ."

Although the estimate on this remarkable letter was only $150, I warned my youthful friend that he might have to go to several hundred, perhaps even more. My most sanguinary estimate proved way off. The boy, bidding at the sale, soon found himself locked in the struggle with a Connecticut millionaire. As the auctioneer called out the bids, one after another the other room bidders dropped out, and at three hundred and fifty dollars only a boy and a tycoon battled for the ownership.

"Four hundred!" shouted the boy.

The millionaire raised a pencil to indicate four hundred and twenty-five.

I could see the youngster lick his lips, and I was quite certain he had committed his allowance far beyond the twelve months on which I had agreed.

"Four fifty," he shouted, waving his catalogue.

Mentally, I had a picture of a youthful debtor mowing lawns during the summer and shovelling snow during the winter.

By now, the duel between the boy and the old man had attracted the attention of the entire gallery. I could hear a murmur in the audience. One man whispered, "Do you think that boy is a shill?"

Up and up climbed the bids. Finally, as though to clinch the matter beyond all question, the boy cried out, "Five hundred and fifty!"

The old man raised his pencil a final time. The fight was over.

In a way, I was happy for my young friend. I knew that he had been crushed under a heavy load of money bags, but I also knew that, had he won, he would have saddled himself with a huge debt which might forever have spoiled for him the joy of collecting and the enormous thrill of bidding at auction.

22

A PEEK AT MY PRIVATE MAIL

The young man put down my catalogue, scowling. He had just read a threatening letter to Abraham Lincoln.

"How do you think Lincoln would feel," he asked indignantly, "if he knew that not only the letters he wrote, but even the most private, intimate letters to him were now fair game for autograph collectors? And how would you like it if somebody were to pry into your personal mail?"

"I don't think Lincoln would mind," I answered. "After all, he had no responsibility for the letters which crackpots sent him. And so far as my own mail goes, I've never tried to hide the fact that I've often been a target for irate collectors as well as lunatics. Take this communication for instance," and I handed him a letter which had reached me only that morning.

"Dear Fanfaronading Pantomimist," it read. "I have perused your 'brush off' with interest. You, sir, and your associates, couldn't possibly do any good for me, anywhere. I submitted a query to your office and you behaved like an illiterate greenhead. You've forfeited the game by 9-0. Use your shotgun verbal broadsides elsewhere . . ."

I explained: "I did nothing more than tell this gentleman that his letter of John F. Kennedy had been signed for Kennedy by Evelyn Lincoln."

Perhaps the young man was right in his view that intimate correspondence ought not to be made public. But since I do not agree with him and have been publishing private letters for many years—without including any letters written to me—perhaps it is time I atoned and revealed some of my personal mail.

I receive an average of seventy-five to one hundred twenty-five letters a day, most of which are simple requests easily processed by my staff. Many of my correspondents write in foreign languages, and the addresses they put on their envelopes test the ingenuity of the post office. "Sir Charles Hamilton, at the Sign of the Golden Quill," reads one envelope. "Mr. Hamilton in New York," says another, which by some miracle of skill on the part of our postmen reached me. There are in my mail the usual quota of letters which beg for funds, make preposterous demands or claims, ask exorbitant prices for autographs, offer facsimiles or forgeries, or shower me with praise or abuse.

Recently I had an offer: "I have a driver's license signed by the original Jeannie Genie. How much will you pay for it? I'll take $50,000 for it. It even has her thumb prints on it."

Another letter offers one-of-a-kind handprints and signatures of film stars at a rental of $125 per week; monthly or fortnight rates lower.

Saddest of all are the letters from those who seek to market their letters of President John F. Kennedy, virtually all of which were signed either by his huge battery of secretaries or by his robot. Typewritten letters bearing the authentic signature of Kennedy are worth today about $75 to $150, but most people have an exaggerated notion of value. One man offers a Kennedy letter at $2500. Another asks $5000. Still another explains that "my attorney advises me that the autograph (a mere signature) may be worth as much as $5000 and not less than $3500." Another writes that she and her husband have a Golden Wedding card signed by Kennedy. "Our reason for parting with it is, we want to return to France to see Venus DeMilo . . . It would seem like a voice from the grave to be able to finance our trip in this way . . ." One of the most heart-breaking letters I ever received was from an old woman who wished to sell a spurious Kennedy letter:

Shortly after the late President Kennedy's book, "Profiles in Courage," was published, I wrote to congratulate him and to tell him how very much I had enjoyed reading it.

I never expected to hear from him but, to my surprise & delight, he dictated a lovely letter containing proof of his beautiful character . . . There was extra warmth in it, especially in the sentence, "Again, thank you for your letter and for the pleasure it has brought me." I brought *him* pleasure! Thank God I did, even it if was brief.

    I have treasured his letter throughout the many years & have it almost memorized. However, I would part with it reluctantly . . . because I'm old & *very poor*. Could he help me from Heaven? To think that his letter might almost save my life is beyond human realization!

    Do you think, Mr. Hamilton, that you could sell it for me for a substantial sum?

I had tears in my eyes when I finished reading this letter. I never answered it, for I couldn't bring myself to tell this sweet old lady the truth—that her treasured letter was signed by machine and was virtually worthless.

Only once have I ever knowingly 'misidentified' a Kennedy signature. That was when a mother brought her little son, about ten years old, into my shop, asking me to look at a John F. Kennedy signature, very obviously signed by a secretary, which her son had received from the martyred President. As I studied the signature I saw the little boy watching me, his lips parted, and with a look half of hope and half of despair in his eyes. "Genuine," I announced. "A superb example, and very rare." The glow that spread over that boy's face will compensate me for the extra weeks I will have to spend in purgatory for that lie.

Among the most interesting—at least, to others—of the letters which cross my desk are those which sprinkle me with vitriol. Last year, after I had sold at auction some letters of Lee Harvey Oswald, a collector wrote me: "Please remove my name from your mailing list. Your latest catalogs suggest that you are more artificer than autograph dealer. I have neither time, patience, nor the money for the kind of tomfoolery you have introduced into the business." And the rare-book librarian of one of the largest colleges in Michigan took a portion of his leisure time, of which I presume he has in every day four-and-twenty hours, to inform me that I was "a disgrace to the profession." When I recently sold some letters of Mrs. Kennedy, a man in Rockaway Beach wrote: "Your selling of the letters of the former First Lady, Mrs. Kennedy, can be closely ranked with their being offered for sale by their owners. This is a mercenary, discreditable act.

"There should be a law to prevent such selfishness and greed. I trust that the public will make you aware of this by not patronizing your establishment."

The onus of this communication was somewhat relieved by another letter in the same mail, praising my stand and urging me to turn my talents to politics where I could serve the cause of the underdog.

Perhaps the most unusual of the letters that I find in my mail are those from the lunatic fringe, many of which offer strange propositions. A lady in Hartford, who had accidentally entangled the affinities of literature, asked if I would be interested "in an autograph of Harriet Beecher Stowe, who was the daughter of Mark Twain." Another woman warned against the activities of Hersz Cukier, Hersz Sztern and Jankiel Totelbaum, which tongue-twisting trio was seeking "to kill innocent people by the use of supersonic waves" that "paralyze and destroy the human body."

Not long ago I received a perfumed epistle which apparently announced the second coming of Christ. I was asked to make a gift of one of my books to the infant, a very flattering request, especially as I have never considered myself to be in the élite class of the Magi. "My daughter. . . . had six dreams of God telling her she would have her last son (two years before he was born) and the date he would be born (he was born on the date God told her). God also told her his name . . . (which they named him) and that he was someday to reveal the glory of God as no other man before him except His son, Jesus, and that in her last days she was to start making a collection of books for him to develop a taste for the thought and ideas expressed by others to help him face the dark of the future. She has asked me if you would please sign one of your books (books make your thinking —and they cannot afford to buy books for him) to their son, as a gift. Do not put his name on the envelop. Put mine, and I will take your book to my daughter to see, and give to her son . . ."

This remarkable communication was still fresh in my mind when I received the only possible letter which could top it—right from the Savior Himself, living in Florida. He wrote: "I am Jesus Christ. I found myself through my Word. Those who know my truth will know me—my sheep know my voice. I am here as an ordinary man. The

Christ of Christianity has descended from the clouds, and Jonah has been released from the belly of the whale. I gave my name and my life to be glorified. Now I accept the power and glory which has been given to my name . . . I should like my trial to be conducted openly so that the ordinary man may be judge and jury of this truth . . . Let those who call themselves Christians arise and be counted . . ."

I am ready to appear with all my saints!

Sincerely,
Jesus Christ

Always amusing are letters of unknowns who seek to sell their own autographs. Two college students in Canada saw my advertisement, reading, "Get the top cash price for your autographs" and flippantly mailed me theirs, ornately scrawled on a sheet of paper. "Let's have your top offer for our signatures."

"They are such distinguished scrawls," I replied, "that I cannot in all conscience pay less than fifty thousand, and I am enclosing payment in this amount." The fifty thousand was an inflated German mark note, of no monetary value, which I had just acquired in a huge collection that morning.

A young soprano in Michigan whose ambition was to join the Metropolitan Opera Company sent me her signature, enjoining me to preserve it because "this autograph will be very valuable to you." And a clairvoyant in Illinois wrote: "I am interested in knowing, not only what profit my autograph would bring me, but also how much profit the autograph would net you. I mean to be fair of equal profits to both of us, or in other words, 50-50 profit to both parties involved . . ."

Perhaps I passed up a good bet when I failed to buy from this liberal gentleman a sheaf of his signatures, which, by the way, he signs with a very bold and convincing flourish.

23

HOW TO COLLECT FOR
INVESTMENT OR PROFIT

"Suppose I want to put my money into autographs instead of stocks and bonds," a wealthy man asked me recently, "just how do I go about it?"

"Buy the best," I told him, "and you can never go wrong. Buy the cheapest and you may lose."

"What do you mean by 'the best'?"

"Everything rare and fine and important—the 'gilt-edged' autographs. If you have a great deal to spend, buy fine letters of Washington, Lincoln, Napoleon, Poe, Melville, Hawthorne. Let nothing good escape you. Pay the top price and get the top material. Of course, if you want to gamble . . ."

"I like to take a flyer now and then," he said.

"Good. Then you might try the new, young people. They may be the Hemingways and Faulkners of tomorrow. Remember Lord Bryon's 'pyramid' in which he evaluated his contemporaries? At the top were Samuel Rogers and George Crabbe, both almost forgotten. In the middle, Thomas Moore and Thomas Campbell, and, at the bottom, Wordsworth and Coleridge. The writers of no importance, like Shelley, Keats and Blake, he omitted altogether. But, in Byron's defense, let me add that he was merely echoing the fashionable critical opinion of his day. So if you like a good gamble, go after Lawrence Ferlinghetti manuscripts and letters. Or collect astronauts. If you lose the gamble, you will at least have had the fun of owning letters of men you admire."

"You haven't told me how autographs compare with stocks and bonds," urged my friend.

"There isn't any comparison. In 1914, a wealthy widow asked for advice from one of the Rothschilds about investing her late husband's fortune. He told her to put her money in German imperial bonds, which he called 'the best investment in the world.' She followed his advice, and in less than five years she had become a pauper. Had she invested her wealth in letters of Martin Luther, Beethoven, Goethe, and other great names of German history and literature, she would have lost not a single pfennig, and in all likelihood would, even in this period of financial chaos in Germany, have substantially increased her modest fortune."

"That's sort of a far-fetched case, isn't it? The disastrous inflation that hit Germany after World War I could never overtake us here. Would you be able to cite any American examples?"

"Well," I told him, "my widowed mother, on the advice of her bank, put her money into what the bank called 'gilt-edged first mortgages,' one of which, I recall, cost her $10,000 in 1929. By 1933, when we desperately needed money, it was valued at only ninety dollars. No fine autographs depreciated to such an extent. I often wished my mother had put her money into G. Washington Preferred!

"Now, if you are inclined to think that those who invest in autographs 'do not understand the value of a dollar on the market,' permit me to name a few investors. There was Henry E. Huntington, who put millions of dollars into autographs and rare books, partly because he was convinced that the stock could never go down. There was J. P. Morgan, who bought manuscripts at such high prices that a lot of wise market owls hooted at him and warned that he would soon be without his great fortune. The manuscripts he bought are now worth fifty times as much as he paid!

"There are others, too, not financial tycoons, but millionaires. Franklin D. Roosevelt put a substantial sum into his autograph collection, and today it is worth many times its cost. John F. Kennedy greatly enjoyed the hobby; and, although he had many other interests and commitments, he delighted in gathering important and interesting autograph letters."

The wealthy, potential collector laughed good-naturedly. "But you're prejudiced, of course. You won't find the Wall-Streeters in agreement with you."

For an answer I pulled an assortment of news clippings out of my desk. "Allow me to read a few," I said. "Here's one from *The New York Times*:

" 'What were the best investments of 1965? Not the stock market generally, although the Dow-Jones industrial averages set an historic high at the end of the year, up about eleven percent from a year ago.

" 'The best investment was unimproved land bordering on large cities, according to Dr. Franz Pick, the money expert, who keeps track of price changes around the world. He reports that land prices rose by eighty to one hundred percent here and in many other nations.

" 'The second-best investment for 1965 proved to be rare books and autograph manuscripts for some lucky sellers who could show gains of as much as eighty percent.' "

The article I showed my friend was typical. Roger W. Babson, the financial expert, in his syndicated newspaper column, recently recommended thirty hobbies among the best investments, including "manuscript and autograph collecting."

My friend quipped: "You seem to have the support of everyone but *The Wall Street Journal*."

"I was hoping you'd bring that up. I just happen to have a clipping here from that very newspaper." I handed him an article headlined on the front page of *The Wall Street Journal*.

"In 1771," the article said, in part, "a Virginia landowner wrote a letter to his brother, Samuel, in which he discussed politics and family matters. 'I cannot help thinking,' he wrote, 'that our Brother Charles is acting the part of a madman to rent his land to people of such force who must, in the nature of things, cut down and destroy his land to all intents and purposes . . .'

"The worried landowner soon would be absorbed in larger problems. His name was George Washington, and the original of his four-page letter to Samuel sold at [Charles Hamilton's] auction for $3,300 last October [1964]. As recently as 1951 the same letter sold for only $125, a price change which reflects the dramatic growth of interest in letters and other papers signed by the famous—as well as by the infamous.

"Charles Hamilton, a leading New York dealer in such material, figures the number of serious individual collectors has increased tenfold in the last decade and now totals about 5,000. He estimates that their spending, together with the amount spent in this field by universities and museums, will exceed fifty million dollars this year . . .

"A number of collectors . . . are greatly interested in potential profits made possible by the rising market. Joseph Schlang, a partner in Schlang Bros. & Co., a building management firm, says he considers investing in autographs just as lucrative as investing in real estate. In the past few years he has put about $35,000 into autographs. He believes the autographs are now worth twice that much, and he intends to keep adding to his portfolio . . .

"For 40 years Nathaniel E. Stein, manager of a New

York branch office of the brokerage firm of Newburger, Loeb & Co., has been keeping a record of autograph prices somewhat similar to stock averages. Mr. Stein says that his charts show a steady, upward movement, even through the Depression."

Speaking of outstanding price increases, of which there are so many that they would cram a volume, I recollect that when I held the sale of the autographs in the collection of Lucius S. Ruder of Clearwater, Florida, the prices fetched were so far in advance of those which Ruder had paid that they left me as well as the audience almost dizzy with amazement. I saw the bidding on a vellum document of Louis VII of France mount steadily until it was knocked down for $1600. It happened that Gordon T. Banks of Goodspeed's in Boston was sitting near me, and among the effects of Mr. Ruder I had seen a bill from Goodspeed's for this very document. I scribbled in pencil on a napkin, "You sold it six years ago for $135," and passed it to Banks. He smiled ruefully, nodding. Doubtless Banks' price was right at the time, but the bull market in autographs makes the purchases of even last year seem bargains.

Lucius S. Ruder, whose autograph collection fetched $382,154 in 1966, was not preoccupied with collecting for profit. He assembled his collection wisely, much as a market investor would make up his portfolio. His Revolutionary generals, Confederate leaders, especially "Stonewall" Jackson and Robert E. Lee, Anthony Wayne, leaders of the Old Northwest, Presidents, and others were truly magnificent. Like a skilled investor, he had diversified his holdings. Except for his Confederate autographs, which fetched only about as much as Ruder had paid, his collections brought prices far in advance of their original cost. It was Ruder's practice to buy fine material at fine prices, never cheap material at cheap prices, and the quality of his collection attracted eager bidders from all over the world.

As an example of the bullish market in really fine autograph manuscripts, I might cite the case of a letter of Washington which I purchased some ten years ago for about $500 from a dealer in Paris. In the letter, Washington, then President, wrote: ". . . .I have no wish superior to that of promoting the happiness and welfare of this Country, so, consequently, it is only for me to know the means to accomplish the end, if it be within the compass of my powers."

At the time, there were many Washington letters available for as little as $100 each, and my outlay seemed not only extravagant but precarious. The letter reached me by registered mail at a small cottage on Lake Sheridan, Pennsylvania, where I was vacationing. The rural mailman asked me for the French stamps. As I opened the package to remove them, I held up the precious letter commenting, "It may interest you to know that you have just delivered a letter written by George Washington in 1789."

For a moment he stared silently, in awe and amaze-

273

ment. Then he whispered, "My God! I knew the mails were slow, but I never suspected they were *that* slow."

This fine letter found no taker when I catalogued it; but Dr. Bernard Pacella, a distinguished New York psychiatrist who recognized its importance, bought it from me for $1000 a few months later. Five years went by, and Dr. Pacella decided to present the letter to the Riverdale Country School, where he felt its presence would be an inspiration to the boys. For tax-deduction purposes, I evaluated the letter at $5000.

Then, about six months ago, the principal of the Riverdale Country School wrote to me, explaining that they wished to sell the letter and that Dr. Pacella had agreed to the sale. Would I put it up at auction for them? I would, and did.

In a fiercely contested battle, Mabel Zahn of Sessler's finally outbid Malcolm Forbes for the ownership of this magnificent letter. I had expected it to fetch upwards of $5000, but I was flabbergasted when it was finally knocked down for $25,000—exactly fifty times the amount I had paid for it a decade earlier. It was a new world's record for Washington.

My advice to anyone who wishes to buy autographs for investment is to follow the pattern set by Lucius Ruder, one of the great collectors of modern times. Diversify, and buy the finest. Never compromise with quality. Thus, if you cannot afford a good Poe letter, buy a good Longfellow letter. If you cannot afford a choice Washington letter, buy an excellent letter of Philip

Schuyler. But do not put your money in mere signatures or insignificant scraps.

A word of caution about collecting modern literary letters. There is today such a frenzy to gobble up manuscripts, whatever their merit, that collectors and libraries are seized by a kind of madness not unlike the tulipomania of several centuries ago, and carried on with even less discrimination. No longer is it necessary for a work of art to survive the crucible of time to become valuable in manuscript form. Today poets sell their manuscripts almost before their books are published. Plays are bartered away as autographs before they are produced. Novelists complain that their private letters are put up for sale almost before the ink is dry.

Manuscripts of fashionable authors almost invariably fetch huge sums at auction. A fair copy (not the original) of Eliot's *The Waste Land,* a poem which has yet to survive the tough test of time, was sold for more than $7000 at a London auction. A zealous collector paid $6000 for a corrected typescript of Tennessee Williams' *The Glass Menagerie.* The University of Texas emerged the victor in bidding for a fragmentary manuscript of Forster's *A Passage to India* at the incredible sum of $16,000. Dylan Thomas' widow recently sued for the recovery of the manuscript of *Under Milk Wood,* valued by her at about $50,000. I turned it down ten years ago when it was offered to me at $2,500.

One British dealer, Alfred Miller, who makes a business of selling modern manuscripts to Americans, reports that many young writers are now making more from their autograph manuscripts than from their publishers. "I recently sold," he commented, "the manuscript of a young unknown's first book of verse for fifty-six pounds." Thus rages the manuscript epidemic; and if the benefits to scholarship are doubtful, at least many popular authors have discovered an easy way to make money.

The intelligent investor will avoid such pitfalls as modern authors and political figures, unless he wishes to gamble—though there are great pleasures in any gamble which pays off. I have been guilty of gambling only twice. The first time I stocked up on letters of Senator Robert Taft who, I thought, was certain to be the Republican nominee for President. The second time I purchased, at handsome prices, large numbers of letters of Thomas E. Dewey who, I believed, was sure to defeat Truman. I was going to be the best-stocked dealer in New York when Dewey took the Presidential oath of office. Eventually I disposed of these speculative investments for about one-tenth of what they cost me.

Whatever autographs you decide to collect for investment and profit, one thing is certain. You can never lose, for your autograph collection will bring you great cultural pleasure. There can be no intellectual joy in assembling a portfolio of stocks, but, in the wonderful field of autograph collecting, you can have your cake and eat it, too.

INDEX

INDEX

278